CONTINUUM CHARACTER STUDIES

OTHELLO
CHARACTER STUDIES

NICHOLAS POTTER

continuum

Continuum

The Tower Building
11 York Road
London SE1 7NX

80 Maiden Lane, Suite 704
New York
NY 10038

www.continuumbooks.com

British Library Cataloguing-in-Publication Data
A catalogue record for this book is available from the British Library.

ISBN: 978-08264-9432-0 (hardback)
978-08264-9433-7 (paperback)

Typeset by Servis Filmsetting Ltd, Manchester
Printed and bound in Great Britain by
MPG Books Ltd, Bodmin, Cornwall

To Ninon

CONTENTS

SERIES EDITOR'S PREFACE

This series aims to promote sophisticated literary analysis through the concept of character. It demonstrates the necessity of linking character analysis to texts' themes, issues and ideas, and encourages students to embrace the complexity of literary characters and the texts in which they appear. The series thus fosters close critical reading and evidence-based discussion, as well as an engagement with historical context, and with literary criticism and theory.

Character Studies was prompted by a general concern in literature departments about students responding to literary characters as if they were real people rather than fictional creations, and writing about them as if they were two-dimensional entities existing in an ahistorical space. Some students tend to think it is enough to observe that King Lear goes 'mad', that Frankenstein is 'ambitious', or that Vladimir and Estragon are 'tender and cruel'. Their comments are correct, but obviously limited.

Thomas Docherty, in his *Reading (Absent) Character: Towards a Theory of Characterization in Fiction*, reminds us to relate characters to ideas, but also stresses the necessity of engaging with the complexity of characters:

> If we proceed with the same theory as we apply to allegory [that a character represents one thing, such as Obstinate in Bunyan's *Pilgrim's Progress*], then we will be led to accept that Madame Bovary 'means' or 'represents' some one essence or value, however complex that essence may be. But perhaps, and

more likely, she is many things, and perhaps some of them lead to her character being incoherent, lacking unity, and so on. [. . .] It is clearly wrong to say, in a critical reading, that Kurtz, for example, in Conrad's *Heart of Darkness* represents evil, or ambition, or any other one thing, and to leave it at that; nor is Jude a representative of 'failed aspirations' in Hardy's *Jude the Obscure*; nor is Heathcliff a representation of the proletariat in Emily Brontë's *Wuthering Heights*, and so on. There may be elements of truth in some of these readings of character, but the theory which rests content with trying to discover the singular simple essence of character in this way is inadequate [. . .]. (1983, p. xii)

King Lear, for example, is complex, so not easily understandable, and is perhaps 'incoherent, lacking unity'; he is fictional, so must be treated as a construct; and he does not 'mean' or 'represent' one thing. We can relate him to ideas about power, control, judgement, value, sovereignty, the public and the private, sex and sexuality, the body, nature and nurture, appearance, inheritance, socialization, patriarchy, religion, will, blindness, sanity, violence, pessimism, hope, ageing, love, death, grief – and so on.

To ignore this, and to respond to Lear as if he is a real person talking ahistorically, means we simplify both the character and the play; it means, in short, that we forget our responsibilities as literary critics. When, for example, Lear cries, 'Howl, howl, howl, howl! O, you are men of stones!' (5.2.255), it would be wrong to ignore our emotional response, to marginalize our empathy for a father carrying his dead daughter; but we must also engage with such other elements as: the meaning and repetition of 'Howl' (three howls in some editions, four in others); the uncertainty about to whom 'you are men of stones' is directed; what 'men of stones' meant to Shakespeare's audience; the various ways in which the line can be said, and the various effects produced; how what Lear says relates to certain issues in the play and introduces new ideas about being human; what literary critics have written about the line; and what literary theorists have said, or might say, about it.

When we embrace the complexity of character, when we undertake detailed, sensitive critical analysis that acknowledges historical context, and literary criticism and theory, and when we relate characters to themes, issues and ideas, the texts we study blossom, beautifully and wonderfully, and we realize that we have so much more to say about them. We are also reminded of why they are worthy of study, of why they are important, of why they are great.

Ashley Chantler
University of Chester, UK

AN OVERVIEW OF *OTHELLO*

Shakespeare's dramatized re-working of a story from Giraldo Cinthio's *Hecatommithi* ('The hundred tales', 1565) does not at first sight seem to fit very easily into the rest of his work. Unlike the other three great tragedies (*Hamlet*, *King Lear*, *Macbeth*), there is no supernatural element, no socio-political crisis, no larger dimension than the intimate intriguing of two or three people. It is a domestic tragedy, unusually closely focused in terms of the characters it introduces us to and unusually 'realistic' for Shakespeare. His decision to make a tragic hero of a 'blackamoor' was a bold reversal of his depiction of Aaron in *Titus Andronicus*. It was given before James I, in the Banqueting House at Whitehall on 1 November 1604.

Shakespeare added Roderigo and Brabantio to Cinthio's characters and named the characters, who are only known in Cinthio by their descriptions (a Moor of Venice; his Venetian wife; his ensign; his ensign's wife; a corporal). He introduced the military action between the Turks and the Venetians, which figures so largely in the first Act. The 1623 folio text is 160 lines longer than the 1622 quarto (smaller and cheaper) edition, adding, for example, Desdemona's 'song of "willow"' (4.3.26) and developing Emilia's role in the last scenes. It is likely that the 1623 version incorporates Shakespeare's own second thoughts and additions. It is beyond the purpose of this introduction to discuss textual editing, but it is worth noting that publishing in Shakespeare's time was not as well controlled by copyright laws as it is now, and it is unwise to assume that a printed text represents the author's determinations.

The quarto texts published during Shakespeare's lifetime vary in reliability and the 1623 folio, which was seen through the press after Shakespeare's death by John Heminges and Henry Condell, members of Shakespeare's company, is widely regarded as the first serious attempt to present Shakespeare's work in an edited form. The edition used throughout this essay is the Arden third edition, edited by E. A. J. Honigmann (1997).

The plot is simple: Iago, for reasons he discusses at some length, decides to sow mistrust between Othello and his new wife, making Othello believe that his wife has betrayed him with Cassio. He succeeds and Othello becomes murderously jealous, killing Desdemona. Emilia realizes what has happened and makes Othello see what he has done; Othello kills himself. What we must consider is how we are to set about making something of this.

There are four ways in which characters are created in a play: what they say; what they do; what other characters say about them; and what other characters do about them. However, what characters do is either reported by them or by others, or decided by actors and directors on the basis of the script with which they are working. Therefore everything about characters arises from the words they are given to say. In reality there is one way in which character is created in a play, and that is by the words.

We should not belittle the importance of what is then done with the words by the theatre company working with them: far from it. Any company working with a Shakespeare play has to rely on its ability to interpret what comes down to it; to consider how it has been worked with before; to make cuts for realistic performance; to interpret what it has chosen to work with. This is creative work of the highest order: but it is still taking its starting point from the words, and that is what criticism must do, in parallel, as it were, with the work of the acting company; distinct from it but not in competition with it.

As critics we shall start with the words, then, but first a note of caution. Interpretation is not a straightforward matter. The words on the page are not a transparent medium through which the meaning can be seen. F. R. Leavis accurately describes the process of reading a poem:

It is in the study of literature, the literature of one's own language in the first place, that one comes to recognize the nature and priority of the third realm (as, unphilosophically, no doubt, I call it, talking with my pupils), the realm of that which is neither merely private and personal nor public in the sense that it can be brought into the laboratory or pointed to. You cannot point to the poem; it is 'there' only in the re-creative response of individual minds to the black marks on the page. But – a necessary faith – it is something in which minds can meet. (Leavis 1972, 62)

I have chosen this description as it stresses two things clearly: one, the artificial nature of writing and reading; and two, the active nature of reading. First, writing and reading involve sets of conventions: the 'black marks on the page' are signs indicating letters that indicate (in combination) words. The black marks are not the words: the phrase 'the words on the page' is a figure of speech. The words occur only in the mind of the reader. Second, the occurrence of the words in the mind of the reader is not a matter of the activity of the writer, still less is it a matter of the activity of the black marks on the page: it is wholly and entirely a matter of the activity of the reader.

I should say in parenthesis that this is also true of listening to spoken words: the sounds an actor makes when speaking the words set out in the script are themselves signs of words, indicating words that only occur in the mind of the listener.

We start, then, with our own perception, our own view of what is being said or done. This is not sufficient, however, because we do not know whether we have properly understood what is being said or done, so we test our perception against other people's perceptions. This may take a simple form, such as asking someone we know, someone with whom we have gone to the theatre to see the play or someone else who is reading the play; or it may take a more complicated form, reading published opinions, books and essays on the play. We must always remember that other people's views are just views. They may be more considered than our own, better informed than our own, but they are just views. What we must do is ascertain whether they are in fact better informed, more considered, more in keeping with the work we are studying than the views we hold or to which we are attracted for whatever reason (as, for example, they may be similar to our own views, or support views on other matters with which we have sympathy). There is no 'right' or 'wrong' view: there is only more or less convincingly argued.

To consider the way in which a play presents to us people and actions is to enter into exactly this process of expressing and testing views. We can show how it is done, and ask what we learn by showing how it is done. I begin with the central character of *Othello*.

CHAPTER 1

INTRODUCING OTHELLO

The play opens on an empty stage. Two people enter, arguing: the first to speak is clearly annoyed with the other man:

> Tush, never tell me, I take it much unkindly
> That thou, Iago, who hast had my purse
> As if the strings were thine, shouldst know of this. (1.1.1–3)

The other (who we now know is called Iago) seems to be trying to calm him down: "'Sblood, but you'll not hear me. If ever I did dream / Of such a matter, abhor me' (1.1.4–5). The first speaker rebuffs him: 'Thou told'st me / Thou didst hold him in thy hate' (1.1.5–6). This is the first appearance of Othello in the play: the third person pronoun, here in the objective case, 'him'. It is significant that he appears as a pronoun: he is the intimate, familiar subject of an intense, angry exchange between the two people with whom the play opens, who does not need to be named by them as they both know of whom they are speaking; they are not talking for us; we are overhearing them.

Indeed we may not know of whom they are talking until Iago concludes a long rant against Othello, who, we learn, has just chosen Cassio as his lieutenant: 'This counter-caster / He, in good time, must his lieutenant be / And I, God bless the mark, his Moorship's ancient!' (1.1.30–32). Othello appears again at lines 39 and 56 as 'the Moor'; at line 65 as 'the thick lips'; at line 87 as 'an old black ram'; at line 110 as 'a Barbary horse'; at line 115 again as 'the Moor'; at line 124 as 'a lascivious Moor'; at lines

134–35 as 'an extravagant and wheeling stranger / Of here and everywhere'; at lines 145, 162 and 175 as 'the Moor'. He himself appears at the beginning of scene 2 but is not named; at line 57 of scene 2 he is referred to in his presence as 'the Moor'. Finally, in scene 3 at line 48 he is referred to again as 'the Moor', though this time as 'the *valiant* Moor [my emphasis]' and the Duke straight-away addresses him directly by his name: 'Valiant Othello, we must straight employ you / Against the general enemy Ottoman' (1.3.49–50).

It is worth reflecting carefully that 329 lines have been spoken and much action has already taken place and information been imparted before anyone uses Othello's name. The implications are clear. We are not surprised that Iago and Roderigo (as we learn the two are called) do not name him because they are both earnestly discussing him; there is no need to name him. However, when they rouse Brabantio he, too, seems to know instantly of whom they are speaking (or rather, shouting: they are standing below Brabantio's balcony) without his being named. Finally, when he appears before the Senate, the First Senator, who announces Othello's arrival, refers to him as 'the Moor' without having to name him. The subtitle to the play tells us why: Othello is 'the Moor of Venice'. This may not mean that Othello is the only Moor in Venice: it only has to mean that he is the one every-one knows you mean when you use the phrase 'the Moor'. It is not necessarily a term of disrespect: – the First Senator surely does not use it so; though, equally, Roderigo and Iago certainly do use the phrase contemptuously. We learn that Othello is dis-tinctive.

If we turn to what is said of him then the picture is further complicated. Iago says:

But he, as loving his own pride and purposes,
Evades them, with a bombast circumstance
Horribly stuffed with epithets of war. (1.1.11–13)

This means that Othello has made a pompous speech, packed with military figures of speech, like a caricature of a profes-sional soldier: vain, absurd, full of himself, showing off. Outside

Brabantio's window Iago's shouted remarks persistently draw attention to Othello's supposed sexual voraciousness and Brabantio quickly broaches his suspicions to Roderigo of witch-craft on Othello's part:

> Is there not charms
> By which the property of youth and maidhood
> May be abused? (1.1.169–71)

These reported characteristics do not immediately fit together: there is no one kind of person easily imagined who would show all these traits. Each is a caricature but each is a different carica-ture: the vain, pompous soldier; the insatiable sexual savage; the wizard. They are caricatures of the outsider but also of a fear-some figure, possessed of dangerous appetites but also of powers. There is a hint here of the position in which Othello finds himself: he is not just an outsider; he is an outsider on whom Venice depends for its protection. This position is tremendously import-ant as it places Othello in a contradictory position, both 'of' and 'not of' Venice. It also places others in contradictory positions: despising him as an outsider; depending on him for safety.

Othello's own first appearance is remarkably low-key. Though he is onstage, he is silent. Iago speaks first at 1.2.1, describing how, incensed as he was by Roderigo's insulting speeches about Othello, he nearly overcame his better nature and attacked him. This is of course the story as Iago is telling it and it is our first insight, and it is a startling insight, into how easily Iago lies. Othello's first words are almost astonishingly undramatic: ''Tis better as it is' (1.2.6). What can he mean? Iago is trying to get him to share in his indignation and Othello remarks non-committally, ''Tis better as it is.' There is no emotion here whatever: no urgent desire to calm down an inflamed loyal companion; no outraged sense of dignity; no hurt; no irritation; no reaction whatever. Iago persists:

> Nay, but he prated
> And spoke such scurvy and provoking terms
> Against your honour,

> That with the little godliness I have
> I did full hard forbear him. But I pray, sir,
> Are you fast married? Be assured of this,
> That the magnifico is much beloved
> And hath in his effect a voice potential
> As double as the Duke's: he will divorce you
> Or put upon you what restraint or grievance
> The law, with all his might to enforce it on,
> Will give him cable. (1.2.6–17)

The pattern is one we have only just witnessed: Iago has goaded Brabantio with insults until he has provoked a response; here he is doing the same thing. The results, though, are very different:

> Let him do his spite;
> My services, which I have done the signiory,
> Shall out-tongue his complaints. 'Tis yet to know –
> Which, when I know that boasting is an honour,
> I shall promulgate – I fetch my life and being
> From men of royal siege, and my demerits
> May speak unbonneted to as proud a fortune
> As this that I have reached. For know, Iago,
> But that I love the gentle Desdemona
> I would not my unhoused free condition
> Put into circumscription and confine
> For the sea's worth. (1.2.17–28)

At this point we must return to what was said earlier about interpretation. What we make of this speech will depend upon what the actor playing Othello has made of it (and on the director's views of the play), or upon what we make of it as readers. In the first case our response will not simply be to accept what the actor has made of it. Interpretation is not solely the actor's domain: the actor must make his or her recommendations in the context of a company preparing a performance. Strictly speaking, we must think of the company's interpretation and of the actor's within that. For it is also true that the actor is not merely a machine performing as dictated by the company (which is only a collection of actors, director, and so on): additionally, the audience interprets the company's interpretation and the actor's interpretation within the company's interpretation. In this the audience may be influenced by the opinions expressed by critics, or by other readers with whom the performance is discussed, and so on. What I now say, then, is an interpretation and must be interpreted by anyone reading this.

In the first place I have already passed off on you an act of interpretation: I have just said that Othello's opening line is devoid of emotion. You must read the line again and decide for yourselves what to make of it. Put yourself in the place of an actor having to deliver the line (remember that it is the first line of a character about whom much has already been said). What emotional state at this point do you (and we must not forget the director and the rest of the company) want the audience to see? And why? What is your reason for wanting the audience to see that state and not another? You will find that you make the judgement by taking into account what has already happened and what is to come and you will be thinking of what will make the most interesting sense of the whole play as it is finally reflected upon by the audience who has just experienced it. Nor will you forget that audiences are complexes of people: individuals who have turned up on their own and couples and groups and all sorts of interactive possibilities. So, which audience? In what condition? Expecting what? To be gratified by getting what they expected or surprised by getting something else?

What we know of Shakespeare tells us that he was a 'man of the theatre', to use a traditional phrase. We may not be able to decide whether or not he meant his plays to be read (we can probably bet that he would not have minded that they were), but we can know that he prepared them at least initially for performance and that he participated in the business of the company in which he was a 'sharer' (that is, which he partly owned, together with other company members) and that he trimmed and adapted them for different performances on different occasions and, again probably, for different audiences.

All this must be kept in mind when we approach the act of interpretation, for whatever we decide a speech means we shall have to be aware that it will mean something else to someone else and neither we nor they are necessarily wrong. Does this mean then that there is no such thing as an incorrect interpretation? That you cannot get it wrong? For if it does then we may ask what business someone has marking our essays or examination answers. This question, though, has to be approached from a different angle than that of whether something is right or wrong.

When an interpretation is advanced, the question that must be asked of it is whether it is adequate. Does it adequately explain what needs to be explained? Or does it leave elements unaccounted for, or imperfectly or awkwardly included? Second, we may ask whether the interpretation is more or less interesting than other interpretations. Is it pedestrian and expected or surprising and unusual? How does it fit in with the rest of what of we are looking at? Does it throw new light on things or merely confirm what we already know? If it is new and surprising, is it merely eccentric and, though fitting the facts, doing so only at the expense of reasonableness?

That diversion must take us back to Othello's first extended speech again and our interpretation of it:

> Let him do his spite;
> My services which I have done the signiory,
> Shall out-tongue his complaints. 'Tis yet to know –
> Which, when I know that boasting is an honour,
> I shall promulgate – I fetch my life and being
> From men of royal siege, and my demerits
> May speak unbonneted to as proud a fortune
> As this that I have reached. For know, Iago,
> But that I love the gentle Desdemona
> I would not my unhoused free condition
> Put into circumscription and confine
> For the sea's worth. (1.2.17–28)

I have already said that Iago is excitedly trying to provoke a reaction in Othello, and Othello does not seem to be rising to the bait. Iago has given up provoking him with tales of Roderigo's insolence and has now turned to trying to stir up anxieties about his marriage: 'Are you fast married?' (1.2.11) means: 'Have you and she had sexual intercourse?' In law at the time a 'consummated' marriage was much more difficult to dissolve than one that was 'unconsummated'. Iago is asking: 'Are you out of the woods yet? Can her father still get at you?' He is also asking a question that will echo throughout the play for, when Desdemona sadly lays out the wedding night sheets on the bed in which she is to be murdered, we must surely ask whether those sheets have seen a wedding night.

This is not just a prurient question, though some critics have said that it is. When Othello kills Desdemona there is a definite relation established in the play between the murder and her sexuality: 'Strangle her in her bed – even the bed she hath contaminated' (4.1.204–05), Iago urges. 'Good, good, the justice of it pleases; very good!' (4.1.206), replies Othello. I shall return over and over again to the disturbing compliance between murderous feelings and feelings of sexual desire as this is presented in the play. You may of course dismiss such thinking in favour of some other theory altogether. That is the freedom of interpretation, and the nature of the study.

Significantly (for the view I am urging) Othello does not answer Iago's question. Othello answers another point, on Brabantio's power:

Let him do his spite;
My services which I have done the signiory,
Shall out-tongue his complaints. (1.2.17–19)

He describes Brabantio's actions (if he is to take any) as 'spite'. He is not, apparently, much concerned. The reason for his lack of concern is that he has standing with 'the signiory' (the oligarchy of nobles that ruled Venice at the time) on account of the 'services' he has done. These 'services' will do his talking for him against any talking Brabantio may do ('Shall out-tongue his complaints'). We may remember 'a bombast circumstance/ horribly stuffed with epithets of war' and think Othello's words so far not very typical of what we have come to expect from him, on the basis of what Iago has said of him. These 'services', significantly, are what he returns to at the end of the play in his last speech: 'I have done the state some service, and they know't' (5.2.337).

It is not fanciful to say that the beginning and the ending of Othello for us as readers and as members of the audience is his 'service'. It is a fascinating word. To 'serve' is to put oneself at another's disposal, to make oneself a 'servant'. It is a crucial element in the 'discourse' of 'feudalism', which is what Marxist historians (and others I should say, but Marxists make a special use of the term) call the period of history between 'antiquity' (the slave-owning economies of the ancient world of Greece and Rome) and 'capitalism' (the financially fluid and industrially-innovative economies of the sixteenth and seventeenth centuries and onwards in Europe). Feudalism is a form of social organisation associated with a code of 'chivalry', the code of honour of the aristocratic knights who ruled Europe in this period and which features in a number of Shakespeare's plays. Othello is clearly drawn to such a vision of military service.

He speaks self-effacingly of his lineage:

> 'Tis yet to know –
> Which, when I know that boasting is an honour,
> I shall promulgate – I fetch my life and being
> From men of royal siege, (1.2.19–22)

The parenthesis is characteristic: there is a slight, contemptuous, ironic note in it, superior and assured. 'I'll tell you all about my ancestors when it is confirmed to me that to boast is honourable activity.' See how the important word 'honour' appears in this contempt for people who show off. We shall also reflect later in the play that we never really hear anything of Othello's background. The great critic A. C. Bradley talked of Othello entering our world mysteriously 'as if from wonderland' (Bradley, 1991, 177). This is not inaccurate: we do not know anything about him. The hints he drops are tantalizing rather than revealing. Eventually, and finally, we may try to sum it all up. He quickly passes on to:

and my demerits
May speak unbonneted to as proud a fortune
As this that I have reached. (1.2.22–24)

'My faults are compensated for by the status I have achieved', which he speaks of as 'proud'. Proud here may mean 'outstanding', but of course pride is a sin in the Christian framework that still dominated European thinking when Shakespeare was working (which does not mean that everybody believed it: it does mean though that everybody was aware of it).

He ends with a statement of his deepest convictions about life:

For know, Iago,
But that I love the gentle Desdemona
I would not my unhoused free condition
Put into circumscription and confine
For the sea's worth. (1.2.24–28)

Two points need to be considered: his emphasis on freedom and his notion of a great price, 'the seas' worth'. This is usually glossed as the wealth that might be dredged up from the sea, but it could be read to mean the worth of the seas themselves: the amorphous, ceaselessly moving and changing vast body of water itself. The imagery of 'house' and 'circumscription' and 'confine' suggests civilization against wildness, and recalls Brabantio's outraged: 'What tell'st thou me of robbing? This is Venice: / My house is not a grange' (1.1.104–05). That is, 'I do not live in the wilderness; I do not expect to be robbed. This is the city; there are watchmen and guards to protect us from this sort of thing.' There are also manners and conventions and rules and laws of course; these may be thought of as the 'circumscriptions' and 'confines' to which Othello submits himself only because he loves Desdemona.

Strictly speaking, the speech is a *non sequitur*: Othello uses the word 'for', that usually indicates the conclusion of an argument, but what he says does not follow from what he has just said. He *seems* to be saying that he is just as worthy a person as Brabantio, and then saying that his reason for saying this is that he would not submit himself to restrictions unless he loved Desdemona: but that does not make sense. What he is actually saying is that he comes from a very different world and would not submit himself to the restrictions of this one were it not that he loved someone who came from it.

The remaining three-quarters of the scene is a series of rapid alterations: first Cassio, accompanied by other officers, enters, all carrying torches. Iago promptly misidentifies them as 'the raised father and his friends' (1.2.29) and encourages Othello to hide. 'Not I, I must be found' (1.2.30) is Othello's immediate reply: 'My parts, my title and my perfect soul / Shall manifest me rightly' (1.2.31–32). Is this merely confidence that he is being maligned or is it more than confidence; perhaps arrogance and even self-satisfaction? Can one speak of one's 'perfect soul' with humility? There may be a suggestion that Othello must be either saintly or rather pleased with himself. Saints generally don't boast of their perfection, as even consciousness of sinlessness may be over-confidence and arrogance.

Having received from Cassio the Duke's urgent invitation to attend the council meeting, Othello leaves the stage briefly to Cassio and Iago, whose hurried conversation is interrupted by the arrival at last of 'the raised father and his friends' (1.2.29). Just as they arrive, Othello re-enters. Iago tries to hurry him away and Othello resists. The two groups confront one another across the stage. Iago, in a brilliant stroke of Shakespeare's dramatic imagination, immediately challenges Roderigo, his confederate. Othello then says the first really striking thing he says in the play:

Keep up your bright swords, for the dew will rust them.
Good signior, you shall more command with years
Than with your weapons. (1.2.59–61)

The other moments have been potential, as it were; this is actual. In his conversations with Iago we have seen a settled will; here we see command in practice. Confident, casually brave, respect-ful. Iago's challenge to Roderigo is spirited and active: 'You, Roderigo! come, sir, I am for you' (1.2.58). No one is supposed to doubt that he is ready to fight. That is bravery of one sort.

Othello's superbly contemptuous remark scorns danger: put your swords away or they will 'rust'. He means that no one is going to fight here: not because talking and peacemaking is better, but because he is so confident that he will easily overcome any opposition that it would be unkind of him to fight.

Brabantio responds by accusing him of witchcraft and offering to arrest him. Othello calmly responds:

> What if I do obey?
> How may the Duke be therewith satisfied,
> Whose messengers are here about my side
> Upon some present business of the state,
> To bring me to him? (1.2.87–91)

Is he playing with Brabantio here? I have seen productions in which a rather unpleasantly superior smirk accompanies these words, as though Othello is enjoying Brabantio's confusion. Brabantio's words reveal that he does not know that there is a meeting, although an officer states that he is sure that Brabantio will be invited. This puts Brabantio at a further disadvantage. Is there a meeting to which Othello has been invited to which Brabantio has not been, either deliberately or through neglect? I have seen other productions in which Othello merely respectfully reminds Brabantio of what he seems sure that Brabantio has only momentarily overlooked in his agitation. These two, quite reasonable, actors' responses to the words they must speak have quite different implications for the character that is being built up for us, in front of us, on the stage.

The next stage on which Othello appears is as it were a double stage: he appears in front of the gathered nobility of Venice, what he calls the 'Signiory', in what is a very theatrical scene, a very staged scene. Of course, everything that happens in the play is staged, because it is a play: but this scene is staged not only by any company that performs the play, but by the characters created by the play, and by none more than the Duke himself. It is an important, complicated and long scene. It is a scene in which all the resources of dramatic verse are exploited, including prose. It is a scene of the utmost delicacy of feeling and tact of ʟesponse and action. It is a political scene in the fullest sense of the word 'political'. Quickly we become aware that the Venetian state is threatened and confused. Othello's arrival is greeted with intense relief:

> FIRST SENATOR: Here comes Brabantio and the valiant Moor.
> DUKE: Valiant Othello, we must straight employ you
> Against the general enemy Ottoman. (1.3.48–50)

The repetition of the form of address, 'valiant', is greatly significant. It is, perhaps, the word we might have used to describe his behaviour in the previous scene, in fact all of what we have seen of him so far (as distinct from what we have heard of him). However, a difficulty immediately arises. Brabantio recounts the tale of his daughter's seduction by witchcraft, and the Duke solemnly promises to punish with the utmost severity whomever is responsible. Brabantio indicates Othello and an extraordinary thing happens: the Senators, in chorus, say: 'We are very sorry for't' (1.3.74). This is extraordinary because the mode of the play so far has been very realistic. Choral speeches, however short, are not very realistic. I have immediately to say that I am using the word 'realistic' in a very loose sense indeed. I mean only that compared with, say, *A Midsummer Night's Dream*, *Othello* is realistic.

This choral utterance marks the beginning of a striking series of scenes within the scene. Othello and Brabantio make their speeches to the assembled senators; the Duke tries to negotiate a settlement; Desdemona offers her testimony; Brabantio gives up; the Duke steps in again to negotiate a settlement. Then the scene changes so abruptly that it comes as quite a surprise. The Duke's settlement is 'political' or perhaps rather diplomatic; it is, that is, an effort to bring about peace, not so much to settle minds. He does it by pronouncing a set of almost proverbial, even clichéd, sentiments in rhyming couplets:

> Let me speak like yourself, and lay a sentence
> Which, as a grise or step, may help these lovers
> Into your favour.

When remedies are past the griefs are ended
By seeing the worst which late on hopes depended.
To mourn a mischief that is past and gone
Is the next way to draw new mischief on.
What cannot be preserved when fortune takes,
Patience her injury a mockery makes.
The robbed that smiles steals something from the thief,
He robs himself who spends a bootless grief. (1.3.200–10)

Brabantio responds in rhyming couplets but making bitter, sceptical remarks that show that he is not convinced in his heart, but
will accept the Duke's composition of the quarrel:

So let the Turk of Cyprus us beguile,
We lose it not so long as we can smile;
He bears the sentence well that nothing bears
But the free comfort which from thence he hears.
But he bears both the sentence and the sorrow
That, to pay grief, must of poor patience borrow.
These sentences to sugar or to gall,
Being strong on both sides, are equivocal.
But words are words: I never yet did hear
That the bruised heart was pierced through the ear. (1.3.211–20)

As soon as the Duke has what he wants, he turns immediately to
matters of the war and speaks in prose. Othello continues in verse
to make arrangements for Desdemona while he is away and there
follows a discussion, into which she intervenes significantly, that
concludes with the agreement that she will accompany him.
Everyone leaves but Roderigo and Iago, who talk briefly, and
then Roderigo leaves the stage to Iago, who delivers the first
of several soliloquies. The scene thus encompasses a range of
modes of expression and varieties of experience, from tense, delicate diplomatic negotiation to the sceptical bawdy of Iago's conversation. In the midst of it stands Othello. He is outlined clearly
by what is going on around him and at last the tantalizing hints
of the scene in which he first appeared seem to be completely
manifested for us.

It is a triumphant moment. At 1.3.75 the Duke invites Othello to defend himself, and he begins:

> Most potent, grave, and reverend signiors,
> My very noble and approved good masters:
> That I have ta'en away this old man's daughter
> It is most true; true, I have married her. (1.3.77–80)

He begins, that is, not only by admitting, apparently, what he is charged with, but doing so with a certain complacency. One cannot imagine a production in which Othello hangs his head, ashamed, at this point. He continues by apologizing for his lack of polish as a public speaker and finally offers 'a round unvarnished tale' (1.3.91) of the events that have led to his marrying Desdemona. He does clearly, however, make the point that he will, in the course of this account, tell:

> What drugs, what charms,
> What conjuration and what mighty magic –
> For such proceeding am I charged withal –
> I won his daughter. (1.3.92–95)

Othello is no guileless innocent. He has defined the charge Brabantio has brought against him most carefully, distinguishing thereby between what Brabantio resents (that Othello has married his daughter) and what he is charging him with, in the hope of getting back what he has lost. The parenthesis, 'For such proceeding I am charge withal', is a reminder to his audience, the senators, that he knows what they should be looking for.

The tale he tells is of wonders. He tells how Desdemona was captivated by the wonders he spoke of, and of how she hinted to him that should he offer, she would accept. His summary is devastating:

> She loved me for the dangers I had passed
> And I loved her that she did pity them.
> This only is the witchcraft I have used. (1.3.168–70)

At first hearing this means only that she fell in love with a hero of romance, and he responded to her feeling for him. Closer examination, upon reading, or seeing the scene again, may make us wonder what basis for a relationship this is. Iago will later say: 'Mark me with what violence she first loved the Moor, but for bragging and telling her fantastical lies' (2.1.220–21), and we must ask ourselves how wrong he is, or indeed whether he is so very wrong at all. Othello's phrase, 'She loved me for the dangers I had passed' (1.3.168), is a subtle one and can be considered at some length. Does he mean what he seems to mean, that it was the adventures he had with which she fell in love, the 'dangers'; was it rather that he had escaped them, 'the dangers I had passed'; what does it mean to love someone for experiences they have had? A question is raised here that will return: to what lengths is interpretation justified in going?

We must be clear at all times about the context within which we are asking the questions. Are we asking what 'Othello' means, as though he were a real person really saying something? Or are we asking what 'Shakespeare' meant by giving those words to the character he was creating? Or are we asking what the words mean without reference to characters or authors? We should perhaps always be asking at all three levels: within the play, seen as the interaction of characters that will act at least to some extent as we expect people to act and react in our own lives around us; outside the play, from the point of view of what we imagine are the creative processes that went into the making of it (and the re-making of it in performance after performance); outside our lives and the lives of those we know and among whom we assume so much and take so much for granted, and from the point of view of what the words *can* mean, or be made to mean. The perspective that this last level offers may seem abstract and even unreal, but it will throw interesting light on what we and others take for granted, and even open up new horizons.

When we ask these questions we are getting to the heart of the creation of character in a dramatic work. If we assume that Shakespeare deliberately composed these phrases for the actor playing Othello to speak, then we may ask whether he meant us to pick up anything about Othello's self-awareness. To put it another way: if we think that someone who said something like this might be suspected of knowing very little about human relationships, then are we justified in thinking that Shakespeare intended that we should think that about Othello? If we think Othello is deliberately presenting himself as a rather simple-minded soldier in order to relieve the listening senators of any anxiety about Brabantio's charge, then are we justified in thinking that Shakespeare intended that we should think that about Othello? When we talk about imaginary people as though they were real people, there is a danger that we get too set in our thinking both about them and about how our impressions have arisen in the first place. If I think something about Othello then I am likely to think that Shakespeare has very cleverly made me think that. Someone else may think something quite different about Othello, but equally well believe that Shakespeare made her think that. Things may get even more difficult: people may hold that Othello is really something other than Shakespeare has made him out to be.

Here we are getting into the difficult territory of intentionality. Shakespeare may have thought he was doing one thing but ended up doing another. Can we call that an unconscious intention? Freud made a useful distinction between 'unconscious' and 'preconscious' on the basis that when recovered material was confronted without any upset then the material could be thought of as preconscious rather than unconscious, and forgotten rather than repressed, but if the subject was upset by the confrontation with recovered material then it was likely to be repressed rather than forgotten, and unconscious rather than preconscious. Would Shakespeare be upset by some of the material our interpretative activity uncovers (or recovers)? Then there is a further question: would it matter? When a writer has written something we may say that their best efforts to make it mean what they wanted it to mean have been exhausted and it is now our turn. They cannot come back and object to our interpretations: they have had their go; it is our turn now. In other words we are not seeking to uncover what the author meant (or, more precisely perhaps, may have meant to mean) but what the text means. Then we are back to whether limits can be placed upon interpretation.

Anyone who has used a dictionary knows that the meaning of words is always other words, and that those words mean other words in their turn. To get words to mean only what you want them to mean is perhaps a fruitless pursuit, and perhaps we should not even be trying to do it. The Surrealists believed that an unconscious element entered into all creativity and should be encouraged rather than otherwise: why should we restrict our inquiries to what Shakespeare meant to mean, even if it made some sense (any sense) to try to do that? Why should we think that 'what it means' is recoverable anyway? Let's imagine another way of looking at creativity altogether; one in which the creative agent does not start out with an idea of what is to be achieved but with something much more like an intuition, or a glimpse of something perhaps; something like the sort of thing aimed at. It may be that a story engages attention; an image might be striking and moving. How can the image and the story be put together? What would happen if I put this with that on the stage? What would it be like if instead of her doing this she did that? If we think of creativity as creative in this strong sense, not as making something to match an idea in your mind but as seeing what happens as you put things together in different ways, then we don't have to worry about intentions any more. We are entering into a continuous creative process that is unbounded and moving continually forward; not seeking to find our way back to some original idea or impulse. Speculation about origins may help us to move forward but it should not become the end of our quest. The only condition I should myself seek not to impose but to recommend would be the reminder that the process is continual, and that much is to be learned from observing what others have made of the inquiry. However, I should not insist, only invite.

Act 1, scene 3 is the first full presentation of Othello in the play. Starting with what has been said about him we get a confusing impression: the title character of the play is being spoken of contemptuously and bitterly by people we have as yet no reason to distrust, an impression that is further confused by the encounter with Brabantio and that is not absolutely contradicted by our first meeting with Othello himself. Although the impressions we have gained are not thereby strengthened, they are not utterly confounded. Finally we see him before the Senate, accused of witchcraft and a key figure in a national emergency. He speaks calmly, with control and deference, and wins over his audience (with the exception of Brabantio to whom we shall return), vindicating the Duke's description of him as 'valiant' and fully confirming the impression that has been growing ever since we first met him.

It is important to take in the dramatic process: the character that is being created for us is being created in a particular way, and that involves prejudice and the confusion of prejudice. We hear of Othello and form an impression before we meet him, only to find that impression confounded. The lesson is that which Jane Austen indicated in the phrase she initially chose for the title of what was to become called *Pride and Prejudice*: *First Impressions*. We are learning something about character: we are learning that people are not always what we think they are. We are learning about the impressions people make on us and on others. We are learning about what people really are.

Here we should reflect that we may not be able to say what people really are. Perhaps we can go no further than saying that this is how they appear to be. Perhaps we can say no more about ourselves either: perhaps it is only safe to say that this is how we appear to be. There is a resemblance between what we say about ourselves and about each other, and what we say about the people we imagine in books and plays. We are ready to give substance to the hints we get in books and plays because that is what we do in our lives: we give substance to the hints that we get from each other and about each other and about ourselves. That is why embarking upon relationships is so hazardous, as Desdemona famously discovers in this play. That is why Shakespeare, equally famously, has Jacques in *As You Like It* describe the 'seven ages of man' (2.7.139–67) and why he has Macbeth refer to life as:

> a poor player,
> That struts and frets his hour upon the stage,
> And then is heard no more. (5.5.24–26)

The image, one of the actor playing a succession of roles, is as effective an image of character in life as it is of characters in books. We must now proceed to a view of Othello that addresses the various roles he has to play.

CHAPTER 2

OTHELLO: A MAN OF PARTS?

Othello appears in various roles throughout the play: as warrior; as lover; as commander; as jealous husband; as murderer. Perhaps the most remarkable feature of this play is the tight focus upon the central character, and the rapid and extreme changes of character through which he is revealed to us. He appears first (as the previous chapter has shown) as misrepresented by his enemies, and as commanding and rather grand. The rest of the play will set up a sequence of events that shows him to us as jealous and murderous. In the middle of this, and often forgotten, is a tremendous tenderness and longing, and we are not allowed to forget for long the soldier, the leader of men, that he has been and can never quite forget having been.

After the scene before the Senate we next meet Othello in Act 2, scene 1 on the quayside at Cyprus, and once again we have to wait before he arrives. The scene is more than halfway through before he enters at line 179, and he leaves at line 211. We might be forgiven for thinking that, in a play called *Othello*, we have not seen all that much of him. We have, however, seen quite a lot of Iago, and we are going to see more of him in this scene.

Montano and three gentlemen, then Cassio, then Desdemona, Emilia and Iago, all come on and talk: about the dangers of the sea voyage; about fears of the Turkish fleet; and about Othello's personal fortunes, contributing to the impression that much depends upon this elusive character. Montano refers, at 2.1.38, to 'brave Othello'. It is worth noting that at the end of Act 1, scene 3, just before Othello and Desdemona leave the stage, a senator accompanying the Duke as they all leave turns to Othello and says 'Adieu, brave Moor' (1.3.292).

This repetition of the epithet 'brave' acts like the repetition of 'valiant' at 1.3.48–49, and imprints itself on the audience's mind as a just description of this figure. Montano's comment that 'the man commands / Like a full soldier' (2.1.35–36) we have already seen proof of ourselves at 1.2.59ff., so this too acts as a confirmation. When he arrives at line 180 of Act 2, scene 1 it is to greet Desdemona as a colleague: 'O my fair warrior!' His speech to her expresses relief and pleasure in a grand manner but with a note of obvious sincerity:

> O my soul's joy,
> If after every tempest come such calms
> May the winds blow till they have wakened death,
> And let the labouring bark climb hills of seas,
> Olympus-high, and duck again as low
> As hell's from heaven. If it were now to die
> 'Twere now to be most happy, for I fear
> My soul hath her content so absolute
> That not another comfort like to this
> Succeeds in unknown fate. (2.1.182–91)

This pattern – a grandiose image followed by a much more mundane remark – is repeated in Othello's speeches (compare 3.3.456–65 or, most obviously perhaps, his last major speech at 5.2.336–54). It is a mark of his particular style and it is worth noting. He stays on stage long enough to give some orders, and then leaves with Desdemona. The next time we see him it is to intervene to quell the brawl that Iago has stirred up and he appears just as he did at 1.2.59ff., and as Montano describes him: that is, as very much in command, but this time angered. He is angered because they have come to Cyprus to settle agitation, not to arouse it, and his speech makes clear his urgent sense of what is required:

> Are we turned Turks? and to ourselves do that
> Which heaven hath forbid the Ottomites?

> For Christian shame, put by this barbarous brawl;
> He that stirs next, to carve for his own rage,
> Holds his soul light; he dies upon his motion.
> Silence that dreadful bell, it frights the isle
> From her propriety. (2.3.166–72)

After a further speech, in which he shows the same command but which contains a deeper warning of the danger of his anger, he demotes Cassio and leaves the stage with Desdemona, who has entered briefly at line 244. Thus is the plot set up.

Act 3, scene 3 is the turning point. This long scene (482 lines) begins with one of Othello's most moving expressions of his love for Desdemona:

> Excellent wretch! perdition catch my soul
> But I do love thee! and when I love thee not
> Chaos is come again. (3.3.90–92)

He ends the scene saying:

> Damn her, lewd minx: O, damn her, damn her!
> Come, go with me apart; I will withdraw
> To furnish me with some swift means of death
> For the fair devil. (3.3.478–81)

What happens between these two speeches is perhaps the key to the play.

It is important to remember that the character of Othello, in the sense of what he is like, what are his characteristic personality traits, is central to the play. A brief summary of the action is given by Lodovico towards the end of the play:

> O thou Othello, that wert once so good,
> Fallen in the practice of a cursed slave,
> What shall be said to thee? (5.2.288–90)

Criticism of the play must at some point approach such a summary and ask: what happened? Is it, as Lodovico says, that

Othello was practised upon by Iago and corrupted from his original goodness? This seems to be much what Samuel Taylor Coleridge (1969) and A. C. Bradley (1991) thought, but F. R. Leavis (1937) rounded on them both, convicting them of sentimentalizing Othello as he painted a much less generous picture of a man too full of himself to be able to pay much attention to anybody else, and too much a soldier to have any idea of human relationships. Leavis's picture matches the text and is argued closely from it, but Bradley's is not really contradicted by the text, although he adds to it and plays down much of it. Then again, we may be sceptical about 'the text' anyway, from two points of view: first, we may say that 'the text' is nothing more than the script for performance as Shakespeare last left it, polished by editors and raised to the status of an authority it simply cannot claim (because it was working notes, not a finished work); second, that we have become more sceptical about 'meaning', as I have already suggested, and about the stability of texts in general. Nonetheless, such arguments do not refute Leavis, or Bradley either: they allow more flexibility but they do not rule out these views. Practically speaking, most audiences want to be able to say something about what they have just seen and will want to ask themselves to what extent, if to any at all, they are prepared to accept Othello's judgement of himself when he speaks:

> Of one that loved not wisely, but too well;
> Of one not easily jealous, but, being wrought,
> Perplexed in the extreme. (5.2.342–44)

Samuel Johnson handled this comment judiciously, saying that:

> Though it will perhaps not be said of him, as he says of himself, that he is *a man not easily jealous*, yet we cannot but pity him when at last we find him *perplexed in the extreme*. (1969, 143)

The picture is of a man who seems to love his wife but ends up killing her, and there are two questions to ask: why does this happen and why does it exert fascination?

The start of Act 3, scene 3 shows us Desdemona, Cassio and Emilia discussing Cassio's situation. Desdemona is promising to do her best for him. As soon as Othello and Iago enter she starts to press his case with Othello and is met with something of a rebuff. It is very important to our view of what happens next how we see this scene. Othello's mood when she leaves the stage is the key to what happens straight after this, for Iago immediately begins to work on Othello. He asks Othello whether Cassio knew of Othello's love for Desdemona when Othello was first wooing her, and when Othello asks why he wants to know Iago makes light of it: but Othello is suspicious. When they first come on stage at line 28 Cassio takes his leave of Desdemona, and at line 34 Iago says: 'Ha, I like not that'. Othello appears not to hear and asks him what he said. Iago says 'Nothing, my lord; or if – I know not what' (3.3.36) and Othello, seeming not to pay this much attention, goes on to say, 'Was not that Cassio parted from my wife?' (3.3.37), to which Iago replies:

Cassio, my lord? no, sure, I cannot think it
That he would steal away so guilty-like
Seeing you coming. (3.3.38–40)

This is not so much to misread Cassio's departure. He has come to persuade Desdemona to try to persuade Othello to change his mind about demoting Cassio: it is not surprising that he is, as he says of himself, 'very ill at ease' (3.3.32). Othello does not seem to notice and indeed when Desdemona immediately tells Othello that she has been speaking to a 'suitor' (3.3.42), Othello asks 'Who is't you mean?' (3.3.44) Here we need to pause. Why should he ask this question this way? Why does he not say: 'Do you mean Cassio?' This is not to indulge in psychological speculation about a dramatic character as though he were a real person: it is to ask what is the effect of that character saying what he says when he says it. The way realistic texts operate is to create the illusion of the reality of the persons created for the reader/audience. Had Othello said: 'Oh you mean Cassio', as though confirming his belief that it was Cassio he had seen (in the face of Iago's denying that it could be Cassio), then the scene would have taken on a quite different aspect. As it is, when Othello says: 'Who is't you mean?', we are justified in thinking that he is leaving room for Desdemona to lie. Had Shakespeare not wanted us to think that then he could have had Othello say: 'Oh so that *was* Cassio. I thought it was. See Iago? Told you!' 'Who is't you mean?' allows us to think that Othello is testing Desdemona. That is, the words allow us to create that character: a character already suspicious, or ready to be suspicious. Different words might not let us do that. Of course we may find other words in the play that will convince us that we have wildly misinterpreted these words, but that is exactly what criticism is about: looking closely and drawing conclusions as we may.

There is another point that must be made. When Iago asks whether Cassio knew of Othello's love for Desdemona and Othello confirms that he did, we may ask why Othello does not refer Iago to what Desdemona has said earlier:

> What, Michael Cassio
> That came a-wooing with you? and so many a time
> When I have spoke of you dispraisingly
> Hath ta'en your part. (3.3.70–73)

Did he not hear?

These are not speculations about 'what happened'. Nothing happened. The play is not a record of something else. These are just words from which we are trying to construct a 'what might have happened' to go alongside a whole set of versions of what might have happened. How would you play this scene? What would you have happen? Would you have Othello not really listening when Desdemona was speaking of Cassio at lines 70–73? Would you have him, on the contrary, listening intently, and then what would you have him do while Iago is asking him about Cassio? Why does he not say, 'Didn't you hear what Desdemona said at lines 70–73?' Perhaps we should say more precisely, 'why *would* he not say . . .' as what we are doing is speculating, piecing together the evidence we have and trying to fill in the gaps. These are the things they say. Why would they be saying them? As soon as we say, 'why *did* they say them?' we are imagining them as

30

though they are, or were, real people. We may not know that that is what we are doing and there is nothing wrong with doing it: indeed, Shakespeare's company would be delighted to think that they had had such success with an audience that the audience was affected as though they had witnessed events really taking place before them. However, critical sense has to draw back a little and look more closely, because that way more can be found.

This is especially true if we think that works affect us more than consciously. If we think that our critical, reflective capacity might be lulled by works or if we think that, as with advertising or political speech-making, we are being worked on, then we will want to be exceptionally alert to what is going on, to the textual strategies deployed, as it were, in the war to capture the hearts and minds of audiences and readers. This warfare may be conducted quite genially, with the best of intentions and even quite openly, but it may be more subtle than that. It may be that the authors, actors, whoever is involved in the creative work, were not themselves fully aware of what was going on, and what might happen. Art is a form of persuasion. When Dr Johnson wisely stated: 'Imitations produce pain or pleasure, not because they are mistaken for realities, but because they bring realities to mind' (1969, 71), he was completely aware that the bringing of realities to mind brought with it an emotional stimulus. Emotional stimulus is the job of art. However, emotional stimulus carries dangers with it: the dangers of not thinking clearly. When Leavis accused Coleridge and Bradley of sentimentalizing Othello, he meant that they had been so taken in by the play (specifically by Othello's own talking about himself) that they had forgotten to think clearly.

I am suggesting that right from the very beginning of Act 3, scene 3, or at least from the moment of his entrance upon the stage, Othello is not thinking clearly. More precisely, I am suggesting that you take this on as a perspective from which to look at the 'what might have happened' that may be built up from the words on the page. What might be happening is that Othello (the character we are building up from paying close attention to the words Shakespeare – let us say for the moment – has written for an actor) may be presented by an actor as someone who is not thinking clearly. Then we need to ask ourselves why it might be that he is not thinking clearly.

When he says:

> Excellent wretch! perdition catch my soul
> But I do love thee! and when I love thee not
> Chaos is come again. (3.3.90–92)

we can recall his speech when he first lands in Cyprus and use Iago's word, 'bombast', as a measure and ask, is Othello not exaggerating a little? Johnson really liked 'Excellent wretch!', and I do too. It is familiar and immediate and spontaneous. It is not polished and it does not draw attention to itself except as being not very polished. The rest is very grand. Now here is a real difficulty. People in the real world who talk like this make us think that they have prepared their speeches in advance, and we tend to think them not sincere. They may be, but we are likely to be suspicious. What we must judge is whether the same effect is being sought here or whether whoever put these words into the actor's mouth just thought that they were really impressive. The way we ask this is to ask 'did Shakespeare intend this?' We do not necessarily mean what this appears to mean. What we mean (or what it is safe to say, at least) is that it is possible to read this one way or another way and we are looking for grounds on which to base an argument that it should be read one way or the other way.

This takes us back to 3.3.34 and Iago's first attempt to stir up trouble: 'Ha, I like not that.' I have said that Othello appears not to hear what Iago has said, but at 3.3.112 Othello says:

> I heard thee say even now thou lik'st not that
> When Cassio left my wife: what didst not like? (3.3.112–13)

So he did hear. This means that we have room for interpretation. Othello appears not to hear certain things. He does this at 3.3.93 when Iago tries to catch his attention after 'perdition catch my soul'. When Othello says 'What dost thou say, Iago?' it implies – or may be taken to suggest – that he is not paying attention to Iago. Such elements allow us to develop hypotheses. A man

displaying this type of behaviour may be judged to be preoccupied. We may go further: he may be preoccupied with suspicions.
These need not be so well formed as to be actual suspicions of
Desdemona's fidelity: they may only be the kind of uncertainties
that arise from not being in practice. Othello has never been
married before. He does not know how to do it. Helen Gardner
commented:

> It is perilous to garner up one's heart in the heart of another
> human being, and whoever does so loses control of his own
> destiny. Passion has its ebbs and flows. The attempt to found the
> social bond of marriage on passionate love is a great adventure
> of the human spirit – an attempt to unite contrary values – that
> brings with it a possibility of agony that those who seek for no
> such unity in their experience do not risk. (Gardner 1968, 12–13)

And it is worth remembering that, if each relationship is unique
(as each person with whom a relationship is entered upon is
unique), no one knows how to do it.

I shall consider this scene from Iago's point of view later, and
it is a scene, ideally, that needs to be thought about from the point
of view of both participants simultaneously. However, it is possible to think about it from Othello's point of view, if not quite
alone, then at least predominantly.

We must always remember that what we know of Iago from his
soliloquies is quite unknown to anyone else in the play. Othello
has no reason to suspect Iago and Iago presents himself as very
unwilling to answer his superior officer's questions. Having
said this, it is notable that when Iago first mentions jealousy
(3.3.167–72) Othello responds with 'O misery!' (3.3.173), and we
may well think that this could mean that he has thought along
these lines already and is having his worst fears confirmed. He
does not act astonished, as though he had had no inkling of what
Iago is talking about. He quickly starts defending himself against
any suspicion that he would be prepared to suffer a life of jealous
suspiciousness: 'No: to be once in doubt / Is once to be resolved'
(3.3.182–83). This is of a piece with his habit of command; it is
a decisiveness that we expect from someone in his position,

although not perhaps under these circumstances, in which it may appear inappropriate. Othello's soliloquy that starts at line 262 seems to indicate that he is now convinced.

The first lines indicate a confidence in Iago that is to the audience quite as horrifying as it is manifestly unjustified, but of course the dramatic irony consists in that gap between what the audience knows and what Othello (and, indeed, everybody else) knows of Iago: in this case, that Othello is making not only a disastrous mistake but a mistake to which he has been carefully led by Iago:

> This fellow's of exceeding honesty
> And knows all qualities, with a learned spirit,
> Of human dealings. (3.3.262–64)

Then Othello says something very beautiful:

> If I do prove her haggard,
> Though that her jesses were my dear heart-strings
> I'd whistle her off and let her down the wind
> To prey at fortune. (3.3.264–67)

It is a complex sentiment, and much depends on the weighting we give key words such as 'haggard'. The metaphor is taken from falconry and sees Desdemona as a hawk incompletely tamed. This may be taken to be an insulting figure of speech for a person, and this interpretation must be considered. However, what he is saying is that if he were to find that she were not after all his by devotion then, even though he felt strongly for her, he would let her go. Then he turns to self-analysis that begins honestly enough but quickly becomes self-pity. His blackness may be a cause of alienation; his lacking the requisite courtship culture may also put her off; his age may offer a barrier to true kinship. The last of these he cannot bring himself fully to admit though, and he cries out 'yet that's not much' (line 270), as though his pride will not let his honesty have its way. Whichever way it is, 'She's gone' (line 271). The finality of this allows us to remember the image from falconry and see in it an honest recognition of what he believes – that she no longer loves him. However, this immediately passes into: 'I am abused, and my relief / Must be to loathe her' (3.3.271–72). This is brutal and vengeful. He then cries out against marriage:

> O curse of marriage
> That we can call these delicate creatures ours
> And not their appetites! (3.3.272–74)

In a spirit that strikingly evokes the attempt by legal means to capture and chain female desire, and therefore equally evokes the fear that female desire is a force that needs to be controlled, the verse counterpoises 'delicate' and 'appetites' in a phrase with an efficiency which is breathtaking. 'Delicate' evokes a certain kind of male desire, an idealization and longing, and 'appetites' evokes gluttony and excess. The paradox of the kind of male desire evoked here is the paradox of the Virgin and the Whore to which feminist criticism has so often referred, and it runs through the play, as we shall see. The reflex of this longing and despair is a brutality almost infantile in its intensity and in its coarseness:

> I had rather be a toad
> And live upon the vapour of a dungeon
> Than keep a corner in the thing I love
> For others' uses. (3.3.274–77)

This evokes the child who would rather destroy something than share it. However, self-pity is at hand to relieve the tension:

> Yet 'tis the plague of great ones,
> Prerogatived are they less than the base;
> 'Tis destiny unshunnable, like death –
> Even then this forked plague is fated to us
> When we do quicken. (3.3.277–81)

This is extraordinary. Othello tries to make himself feel a little better by reflecting that being cuckolded is after all what 'great ones' inevitably suffer. Thus though he is cuckolded, which is a disgrace, he can comfort himself that "Tis the plague of great ones' and that he is, therefore, a 'great one' too.

Emilia and Desdemona enter and all this is swept aside:

Look where she comes:
If she be false, O then heaven mocks itself,
I'll not believe't. (3.3.281–83)

Desdemona drops her handkerchief; Emilia picks it up; Iago takes it from her and tells us what he going to do with it, usefully reminding us of the nature of jealousy:

Trifles light as air
Are to the jealous confirmations strong
As proofs of holy writ. (3.3.325–27)

It is very difficult at this moment in the play to deny that Othello is jealous, and much that happens from now on is only going to make it harder still. Yet for many critics (Coleridge, and Bradley, especially) this was a road down which they could not go. Helen Gardner speculated that sexual jealousy was too offensive a motive for them to be able to think that a play founded upon it could ever be considered a tragedy. Here we get into the difficult business of trying to determine what makes a play a tragedy.

Aristotle believed that a tale relating misfortune that befell a good man excited only pity, while a tale relating misfortune that befell a bad man only excited a sense of justice. However, a tale of misfortune befalling a man not wholly good and not wholly bad excited the specifically tragic feeling, as long as the balance of vice and virtue were correctly observed. Specifically, Aristotle urged the doctrine of tragic flaw, a failing in the otherwise blameless character of the hero who, finally, should be a man of good standing in society.

The difficulty such critics as Coleridge and Bradley had with *Othello* is that it seems to be a play about a man who is persuaded into a jealous rage in which he kills the woman he has only just married, and that it is difficult to impute to such a man any motive other than sexual jealousy. Such a motive is disreputable

36

in itself, however understandable in some circumstances it may be, and it cannot excite any sympathy as a cause for killing anyone, let alone someone who has done nothing. We may understand, however reluctantly, but we are not going to condone; and although the pathology of feeling may be of interest, it is not going to elevate or edify as an example brought before us. One may ask, as Thomas Rymer famously did, what business it has being on the stage at all. Is it just a lurid horror tale indulging our worst predilections for gossiping and gawping? If there is a rejoinder then it must come from the character of Othello. He must be more than he appears to be.

Unfortunately, nothing Othello does between the end of Act 3, scene 3 and the end of the play encourages hope of success in this endeavour. He demands proof from Iago; he engages in an unholy bond with Iago ('Now art thou my lieutenant' (3.3.481)); he toys hideously with means for Desdemona's despatch (4.1.201–03); he torments Desdemona with the loss of the handkerchief in a particularly ugly scene (3.4.36–99); he falls down in a fit (4.1.43); he snoops at Iago's instigation on a conversation between Iago and Cassio, which he believes is about Desdemona (4.1.93–166); he strikes Desdemona in public (4.1.239); and in 4.2.25–96 he interrogates Desdemona in a scene in which the contrast between the language of religion and the language of the brothel contrast almost unbearably for the audience, who knows that Desdemona has done nothing. The next chapter will consider how Othello appears in the play's closing moments.

CHAPTER 3

OTHELLO: 'SPEAK OF ME AS I AM'

As we approach the end of the play we approach the necessary final judgement: who *is* Othello?

He disappears from the play for two crucial scenes: one between Desdemona and Emilia, as Desdemona gets ready for bed; the other an action scene (into which Othello makes a brief appearance unseen by those on stage), in which Cassio is wounded and Iago disposes of Roderigo. When Othello comes to kill Desdemona it is with a deeply unsettling mixture of emotions that he approaches his task:

> It is the cause, it is the cause, my soul!
> Let me not name it to you, you chaste stars,
> It is the cause. Yet I'll not shed her blood
> Nor scar that whiter skin of hers than snow
> And smooth as monumental alabaster:
> Yet she must die, else she'll betray more men.
> Put out the light, and then put out the light!
> If I quench thee, thou flaming minister,
> I can again thy former light restore
> Should I repent me. But once put out thy light,
> Thou cunning'st pattern of excelling nature,
> I know not where is that Promethean heat
> That can thy light relume: when I have plucked the rose
> I cannot give it vital growth again,
> It needs must wither. I'll smell thee on the tree;
> O balmy breath, that dost almost persuade

Justice to break her sword! Once more, once more:
Be thus when thou art dead and I will kill thee
And love thee after. Once more, and that's the last.
            He [smells, then] kisses her.
So sweet was ne'er so fatal. I must weep,
But they are cruel tears. This sorrow's heavenly,
It strikes where it doth love. She wakes. (5.2.1–22)

This is another speech that needs the closest attention. The accents of desire are unmistakable (we remember that Othello had said that he would poison her 'lest her body and beauty unprovide my mind again' (4.1.202–3)), especially in the repeated 'once more' and the futile attempt at self-restraint: 'Once more, and that's the last.' There is odd mention of justice and the strange self-deception that he is doing this reluctantly on behalf of others ('Yet she must die, else she'll betray more men'). He is clearly confused. I shall return to this speech in Chapter 5 to discuss it more fully than is required at this point.

When Desdemona wakes Othello is brusque and brutal, forgets his promise to let her pray, and stifles her in a cold fury. He comes to his senses in a moment that the critic F. R. Leavis characterized, not unjustly, as 'an intolerably intensified form of the common "I could kick myself"' (Leavis 1937, 273), and then he kills himself, having made a speech in which T. S. Eliot was sure he could hear him 'cheering himself up' (Eliot 1951, 131).

F. R. Leavis described Othello's death scene as a *'coup de théâtre'*, and further asked 'Who does not (in some moments) readily see himself as the hero of such a *coup de théâtre*?':

> That he should die acting his ideal part is all in the part: the part is manifested here in its rightness and solidity, and the actor as inseparably the man of action. The final blow is as real as the blow it re-enacts, and the histrionic intent symbolically affirms the reality: Othello dies belonging to the world of action in which his true part lay. (Leavis 1937, 275)

F. R. Leavis's essay is an answer back to critics such as Coleridge (1969) and Bradley (1991), who had explored the play as the depiction of a character and had looked for psychological coherence that would satisfy their sense of the goodness of the character; F. R. Leavis presents a very different psychological coherence because he is not so convinced of the goodness, at least of the *nobility*, of the character, as Coleridge and Bradley were. In Leavis's view, what Shakespeare has created is a rather simple character, given to self-dramatization, unwise about human relationships, essentially either pleased with himself, or sorry for himself – or, in this last speech, both.

What these views share is the pursuit of psychological coherence. The question they answer is, what kind of man is Othello? Leavis notes that he is not a man at all but a dramatic creation, yet he does implicitly acknowledge that a psychologically-coherent picture is required.

This is, of course, to present what I shall call a 'psychological' description: it describes Othello and the action of the play as though what was being evoked for us was a man and a set of actions performed by people and acting upon people. If *Othello* were a history – not a 'history play', but a proper history – that is exactly what we should expect: but this is a play, and there neither is nor was such a person as Othello. Such reflections do not allow us to act as though no one were being evoked for us, no people and no actions performed by and affecting people: there is no sense in an approach to a play that merely denies what it is apparently showing. Such reflections do, however, encourage us to think more widely than merely 'psychologically', and the golden rule here is that if we put the effort in we shall get more out.

Characters may reveal characteristics, and characteristics have a special status in culture. The ways in which we describe character (in life as in literature and theatre) are taken from the lexicon of values and determinations ('facts') of which a culture is composed. Literature and theatre allow us to look at what we do in our culture, giving us, as it were, some distance between what we do and the picture we present to ourselves of what we do, not only in literature and in theatre but elsewhere as well, in art, cinema and television, and so on.

A useful insight into the nature of culture derives from the linguistic researches of Ferdinand de Saussure. In this view, meaning is produced by language, and language is a system of differences. That is, it is a system of signs (things that stand for other things) that work as signs because they are distinct from one another. Signs have two aspects: 'signifiers' (the material aspect of a sign) and 'signifieds' (the mental aspect of a sign). A differential set of sounds ('signifiers': the material aspect of a sign) is generated to match a differential set of meanings ('signifieds': the mental aspect of a sign). Each individual 'signifier' has meaning because it is distinguished from similar signifiers, and is used within a language to designate a particular signified (thus, for example, 'cap', 'cat' and 'bat' are similar sets of sounds with widely different meanings). A particular signified has meaning as it is distinguished from other similar signifieds (thus 'cap' is distinct from 'hat'). It should be emphasized that signifieds are not things in the world but ideas of things: so 'cap' or 'hat' is no particular item of headgear, but the *idea* of such items. It is 'unlikeness' to anything adjacent (and therefore similar enough for confusion to arise between them) that distinguishes one thing from another thing in this phonological universe and its equivalent mental universe.

This is particularly important in cases of 'oppositeness'. So to take a set of terms extremely significant to *Othello*, 'black' is not 'white'. But if 'black' is not 'white' then 'white' is not 'black', and so 'black' is not 'not-black' and 'white' is not 'not-white'. In other words they need each other to define themselves; they do not define themselves by themselves.

However, if this is so, then the terms 'black' or 'white' can always be substituted by the terms 'not-white' and 'not-black', and we get statements such as 'not not-not-white' for 'white', and so on *ad infinitum*, because how could you ever find a form of words that would finish?

Complexity can increase. When the Duke says 'Your son-in-law is far more fair than black' (1.3.291), he is saying (among other things) he is more 'not-black' than 'black' or, we might say, 'more not not-not-white', just to show how confusing this could become. When we add that there is pun on 'fair', so that it doesn't just mean 'white' (which would be a startling paradox – an oxymoron) but means 'just' (which goes some way to explaining the paradox as a mere paradox and not an oxymoron), then we suspect a rhetorical dodge – as Brabantio does throughout this scene.

In this way 'otherness' – sometimes called 'alterity' – can be seen as a definitive principle. Without clearly distinct 'otherness', we may not define anything. This has a political dimension: how can we define an 'us' if we do not have a 'them'? It has also a psychological dimension, as sameness is reassuring but difference may be exciting. When we approach the social organization of desire, and of sexual desire specifically, then we can see how this principle becomes a useful analytical tool. We can consider heterosexuality as a sexuality of the 'other' (the prefix 'heter-' or 'hetero-' comes into English from an early French derivation from late Latin from the Greek, and is used to form words in which it signifies 'otherness' or 'difference'), but where does 'otherness' stop? When Othello uses phrases such as 'the flinty and steel couch of war' (1.3.231) and contrasts this with a 'thrice-driven bed of down' (1.3.232) and refers to 'the soft phrase of peace' (1.3.83), and later to 'soft parts of conversation' (3.3.268), we start to associate Othello with hardness and Venice with softness. He is 'unrefined' and Venice is 'refined'. However, we remember Brabantio's agony that he has paraded all the 'wealthy, curled darlings of our nation' (1.2.68) before Desdemona and to no avail. It begins to look as though she is getting what she wanted, and that is 'different'. We may start to discuss *Othello* as a dialogue with alterity.

It is, however, vital to stress that these things are problems for *thought*. It is when we try to make sense of the world that we come up against them. Were it possible simply to *live* in the world then we should not.

Valerie Traub (1992) takes a very different view from that of Bradley and Coleridge, and, further, to that of F. R. Leavis. It is in such analysis as Traub subjects *Othello* to that we find the key relationship between character and characteristics developed further, to bear much interesting fruit.

In Traub's view, a dramatic work becomes a screen onto which is projected the key elements of the central conflicts in a culture at the time of the production of the work. The characters are almost devices through which these conflicts are presented and their contradictions articulated. It is to be emphasized that this way of reading is almost deliberately misreading: it is a deliberate attempt to see what the text is trying to conceal, and to show up the joins and the cracks that the work is seeking to smooth over into an integrated and coherent work of art.

The joins and cracks do not appear because of any supposed inadequacy on the part of the artist, but because the ideas that must be presented are themselves incoherent and contradictory. Central to such readings is the belief that the network of ideas with which a society binds itself together is inevitably incoherent and contradictory, because such a network is always the attempt of those with power to convince themselves and others that their power is legitimately grounded and exercised. Thus the attempt to justify a patriarchal society is founded on the distinction between the masculine and the feminine, but, as Shoshona Felman suggests, the feminine will not stay 'outside the masculine [. . .] its reassuring canny *opposite*' but is always found 'inside the masculine, its uncanny *difference from itself*' (Felman, 1981: 41). The distinction is false and cannot be maintained.

Central to Traub's reading of *Othello* is the curious figure in Othello's speech at the beginning of 5.2, when he comments on Desdemona's skin: 'That whiter skin of hers than snow / And smooth as monumental alabaster' (5.2.4–5). Traub links this to a process in Shakespeare's plays whereby women are transformed from being warm to being cold:

> For women in Shakespearean drama, 'chastity' requires being still, cold, and closed; to be 'unchaste' is to be mobile, hot, open. What is striking is the minimal room within which to manoeuvre; even a minimum of erotic 'warmth' is quickly transmogrified into intemperate heat. Indeed, what the drama enacts is the disappearance of any middle ground, with the rigidity of this bifurcation following a unidirectional narrative: from a projection of too much movement, warmth, openness, to an enclosing fantasy of no movement or heat at all. (Traub 1992, 28)

We may remember Desdemona's hand at 3.4.38:

This argues fruitfulness and liberal heart:
Hot, hot and moist. This hand of yours requires
A sequester from liberty, fasting and prayer,
Much castigation, exercise devout,
For here's a young and sweating devil, here,
That commonly rebels. (3.4.38–43)

From this point of view female desire is both desired as a gratification of male fantasy and feared as a fulfilment of the other side as it were of the same male fantasy. It is a force to be disciplined and contained in a society in which men seek to maintain a superior position, and fear to lose this.

It is not being argued that Shakespeare is presenting this: at least not he is presenting this consciously and deliberately. He is producing a work in his time which is marked by his time, and which can be read by a later time as being so marked. How this will affect our understanding of the other characters created by the play will be the subject of the remaining chapters of this essay.

Traub explores not only the paradoxes of sexuality as they impinge upon the Shakespearean world but also, equally importantly, the paradoxes of race. She notes that 'one of the tragedies of the play is the extent to which Othello internalizes their negative representations of his race'. Traub points out that:

In the first three scenes, the discourses of Iago, Roderigo, and Brabantio set up the following dichotomy: black, dark, evil, animal, hyper-sexual, versus white, fair, virtue, human, chastity. (Traub 1992, 36)

She notes that: 'The terms by which Brabantio expresses his refusal to believe in Desdemona's willing love for Othello – "For nature so preposterously to err" (1.3.63) – underscores their culture's appeal to "nature" as the causal basis of these dualisms' (Traub 1992, 36). We may add that the turning point in Act 3, scene 3 may well come when Othello says: 'And yet how nature, erring from itself' (3.3.231), repeating Brabantio's words earlier: 'For nature so preposterously to err' (1.3.63). Martin Orkin

(1987) has argued that much of the play resists this identification of racial prejudice with 'nature', Desdemona's love and Othello's own character at its best being the most compelling elements.

Traub paints a persuasive picture of the character of Othello in terms of a view of subjectivity that takes us away from older views of what 'character' was like, whether in actual human beings or as they were created for us by imaginative works: 'His inability to maintain trust in Desdemona is directly related to his inability to trust his own racial identity and self-worth [. . .] In short, Othello's anxiety is culturally and psychosexually over deter-mined by erotic, gender, and racial anxieties' (Traub 1992, 37). She adds to this his role as a military commander which, she argues, sets up an opposition between order and chaos: we have already seen how Othello uses his authority to impose order upon chaos, in Act 1, scene 2, and again in Act 2, scene 3, Traub argues that Othello associates romantic love with calm and its loss with chaos ('Excellent wretch! perdition catch my soul / But I do love thee! and when I love thee not / Chaos is come again', 3.3.90–92): but 'throughout the play, Othello also equates Desdemona's sex-uality with chaos and violence' (Traub 1992, 37). Thus:

A disjuncture [. . .] exists within Othello's psyche between romantic love (associated with stasis and calm) and sexuality (associated with chaotic violence). Such hostilities, brought to a head by the consummation of his marriage, between the psychic structures necessary to his sense of self and those related to his sexuality must ultimately be reconciled if Othello is not to go mad. (Traub 1992, 37)

This sort of discussion moves some way beyond the search for principles of psychological coherence and analyses of behaviour from the point of view of morality that we associate with the crit-icism of Coleridge and Bradley, and it moves beyond the recog-nition that characters are functions in dramatic experience that F. R. Leavis stressed in his rejoinder to these two. It must be stressed that the development of a critical point of view does not necessarily rebut an earlier view, and indeed may better be seen as refining it. Traub's view does not do away with the search for principles of psychological coherence and analysis of behaviour from the point of view of morality: it adds to it. In adding to it such developments may well also correct elements of it, degrading some emphases and upgrading others. In particular, what Traub's discussion (and others like it) introduces is a sense of character as something other than the integrated, morally responsible and psychologically stable ideal to which so many earlier discussions of character refer.

Character after the twentieth century is much more likely to seem fragmentary, *ad hoc*, interim and ill-understood, and the morality by which its actions are to be judged is much more likely to be severely qualified by a sense of the ineluctable forces whose conflicts drive our culture and which are not, by and large, open to scrutiny in the ordinary way. This may have to do with the discoveries of psychoanalysis, of feminist criticism, Marxism or structuralism, as they have helped to undermine the intellectual conclusions of an earlier age. It also has to do with the catastrophe of the twentieth century, in which the technology that promised a liberation of human beings from drudgery turned genocide into an industrial process, created nuclear weapons and precipitated what may be an environmental crisis. Just as human beings appeared to some to be about to achieve a final harmonization of wants and capability, something seemed to go horribly wrong. The dream of a rational man, equipped with the technology his reason had developed, setting about shaping the world to meet his needs, which were themselves restrained by reason, was replaced by the nightmare of unreason, its capacity terribly extended and its hunger seemingly without limit.

These reflections recall Lodovico's terrible words describing Iago at the end of the play:

> O Spartan dog,
> More fell than anguish, hunger, or the sea,
> Look on the tragic loading of this bed:
> This is thy work. (5.2.359–62)

Lodovico's imagery conjures unlimited appetite: 'more fell than anguish, hunger or the sea'. The things he adduces as parallels to

Iago are almost abstractions, shapeless, boundless. They suggest a view of Iago as almost a natural force, or, perhaps, a supernatural force: and it is to a consideration of this character that the following chapter addresses itself.

CHAPTER 4

IAGO: CHARACTER

Coleridge famously described Iago in terms of 'motiveless malignity':

> The last speech [of Act 1], Iago's soliloquy, shows the motive-hunting of motiveless malignity – how awful! In itself fiendish; while yet he was allowed to bear the divine image, it is too fiendish for his own steady view. He is a being next to devil, only *not* quite devil – and this Shakespeare has attempted – executed – without disgust, without scandal! (Coleridge 1969, 190)

Coleridge's enthusiasm is a useful reminder of the challenge to more modern readings presented by the figure of Iago in the play. His vision is not without warrant in the play. For example: 'If sanctimony, and a frail vow betwixt an erring barbarian and a super-subtle Venetian, be not too hard for my wits and all the tribe of hell, thou shalt enjoy her' (1.3.355–58). And later: 'I have't, it is engendered! Hell and night / Must bring this monstrous birth to the world's light' (1.3.402–03). At 2.3.345 he seems to be invoking a diabolic master:

> Divinity of hell!
> When devils will the blackest sins put on
> They do suggest at first with heavenly shows
> As I do now. (2.3.345–48)

There is even an ambiguous moment in the last scene, in which it appears to be being suggested that Iago might not be entirely human. Othello says:

> I look down towards his feet, but that's a fable.
> If that thou be'st a devil, I cannot kill thee.
>   [*Wounds Iago*]
> LODOVICO: Wrench his sword from him.
> IAGO: I bleed, sir, but not killed. (5.2.283–85)

Does this mean that a more credulous age than ours might have gone away wondering whether Iago really was some sort of devil?

Coleridge does not really mean that Iago is a supernatural being. He means that Shakespeare has presented us with a human being so far removed from the concerns that usually have some hold over the rest of us, however attenuated that may be, that he strikes us as being removed from us. This is especially ironic as Iago clearly imagines himself to be very like us. He talks more than almost any other character in Shakespeare (with the exception of Hamlet), and his talk is frequently directed to the audience, in soliloquies of a very intimate conversational nature. The nature of soliloquies is often ill-understood and therefore difficult to get right, but in Iago's case there is no difficulty at all, as we shall see.

The opening argument is dramatically arresting: we do not know what is going on or who is being talked about, but we pick up instantly some important hints about other things. Roderigo's words, the opening words of the play, introduce Iago as effectively as they introduce Roderigo himself, and they provoke Iago's fascinating response, his opening words. Roderigo says:

> Tush, never tell me, I take it much unkindly
> That thou, Iago, who hast had my purse
> As if the strings were thine, shouldst know of this. (1.1.1–3)

The word 'unkindly' reminds us of 'kin' and 'kind' and 'kindness' as the appropriate form of behaviour towards one's own kin, and so on, but Roderigo follows straight on with the key word, 'purse'. This may only mean a practical form of generosity, or 'kindness', but the curious fact about money is that, unlike other forms of kindness, it is infinitely convertible. If I help someone out by joining in a labour they are undertaking, then that is generous, but they can't take that generosity and do anything else with it; it is absorbed, as it were, in the completion of the task. If I give someone some money to help them out, then they may do with it something other than that for which I supposed they needed it. A relationship built upon money is open to suspicion. As Roderigo is accusing Iago of behaving 'unkindly' when he has been in receipt of generous subsidies we may jump to the conclusion that Roderigo feels he has been used.

Iago responds: "Sblood, but you'll not hear me. If ever I did dream / Of such a matter, abhor me' (1.1.4–5). Coleridge is interesting on this exchange:

> The admirable preparation, so characteristic of Shakespeare, in the introduction of Roderigo as the dupe on whom Iago first exercises his art, and in so doing displays his own character. Roderigo is already fitted and predisposed [to be a dupe] by his own passions – being without any fixed principle or strength of character (the want of character and the power of the passions, like the wind loudest in empty houses, form his character) – but yet not without the moral notions and sympathies with honour which his rank and connexions had hung upon him. The very three first lines happily state the nature and foundation of the friendship – the purse – as well as showing the contrast of Roderigo's intemperance of mind with Iago's coolness, the coolness of the preconceiving *experimenter*. The mere language of protestation in
>
> If ever I did dream of such a matter,
> Abhor me –
>
> which, fixing the associative link that determines Roderigo's continuation of complaint –
>
> Thou told me thou didst hold him in thy hate –
>
> elicits a true feeling of Iago's – the dread of contempt habitual to those who encourage in themselves and have their keenest pleasure in the feeling and expression of contempt for others. (Coleridge, 1969: 186–7)

Coleridge is not easy reading, but this passage repays careful re-reading as it is so packed with ideas. This is perhaps the furthest extreme to which psychological analysis of character in drama can go. Taking a handful of words, and those the first in the play, Coleridge builds an elaborate network of inference reaching into the deepest motivations a person may have, unbeknown to them and unconsciously as it were, with a bold confidence that is repaid by the reader's recognition that, tried out on the play, these sketches will actually work and illuminate much of what happens subsequently.

Coleridge's comments on 'If ever I did dream / Of such a matter, abhor me' (1.1.4–5) are brilliant. What is the worst that Iago can envisage? To be abhorred. He picks up the theme immediately after Roderigo's response, 'Thou told'st me thou didst hold him in thy hate' (Coleridge's 'associative link' – 'abhor' with 'hate'): 'Despise me / If I do not' (1.1.6–7). To be despised is the worst thing Iago can think of. He is trying to convince Roderigo that he has not betrayed him after all, and he is saying 'do the worst thing to me if I'm lying to you', and that is what is revealing because the 'worst thing' for Iago, we now see, is to be abhorred. Coleridge jumps to the psychological assertion that the persons who most hate and fear being abhorred and despised are those who abhor and despise others (though we may quickly say that though no one perhaps very much enjoys it, it is especially the dread of those who tend to enjoy doing it). Is this true? How can we know? Such psychological insights persuade us of their truth because they seem to fit in with ideas we have about character in the persons we know and in persons in general: human character, we may say. What if we know someone who is not like this? We tend to say that they are exceptional. What if we do not believe in this sort of character description at all? Then we shall not believe this particular assertion. In other words, we believe it if it conforms to what we already think, and if we find ourselves believing it without recognizing that it conforms to what we already think then we will have found out something about what we think. Good criticism, like other kinds of good writing, does this.

Whether we want to accept a particular version of human character in general, however, or not, we may readily accept that there is at least one person of whom this description is true, and that is Iago.

The soliloquy towards which Coleridge points us is indeed an extraordinary affair. It is placed at the end of an extraordinary scene, the trial scene, at which we have already looked from the point of view of Othello. Iago does not figure in this scene at all from his entrance with Othello at 1.3.48 to his exit at line 124, with the Duke's officers, to bring Desdemona before the Senate, whereafter he remains silent from his re-entrance with Desdemona at line 170 to the exit (after everyone else apart from Iago and Roderigo) of Othello and Desdemona at line 301. It is important to remember that for a good part of this scene, this riveting, dramatically intense scene, Iago is silently present or else on Othello's errand, and Othello's last words to him are a command:

> Honest Iago,
> My Desdemona must I leave to thee:
> I prithee, let thy wife attend on her
> And bring them after in the best advantage. (1.3.295–98)

The conversation that then ensues between Iago and Roderigo is as riveting as what went before. It is in prose, whereas most of what precedes it was in verse, even in rhyming couplets, and the difference is marked. Just as the Duke turned to prose to get on with the business at line 222, the scene as a whole now turns to prose to get on with another kind business, a cynical, reductive account of human being, courtesy of Iago. Roderigo complains that he will die of love for Desdemona, and Iago scoffs at him. Roderigo admits that it is a weakness to be 'so fond' but claims that it is not in his 'virtue' to change. Iago explodes: 'Virtue? A fig!' (1.3.320) and expounds a view of human being as poised between what he calls 'reason' and 'the blood and baseness of our natures' (1.3.329). In this view 'we have reason to cool our raging motions, our carnal stings, our unbitted lusts' (1.3.331–32), of which, he adds, he regards what Roderigo calls 'love' as 'a sect or scion' (that is, a cutting, or an offshoot, an image taken from gardening).

We need to pay careful attention to what Iago calls 'reason'. When Roderigo denies that love is merely as Iago has described it, Iago replies: 'It is merely a lust of the blood and a permission of the will' (1.3.335–36). Iago is saying, in effect, that when you strip away all the incidental material, the poetry, the rhetoric, the manners, the pretensions, what you have is 'a lust of the blood and a permission of the will'. Iago is being reductive. Now there is an approach to things that is rightly called reductionist: that is what science does. Stripping away what is incidental, what is not necessarily a part of a thing, science seeks to show what must exist as a minimum qualification for a thing to be what it is. In this respect what Iago is doing may seem to be scientific. He is stripping away pretension. We may see this as a determination to see what is really going on under a veil of illusion. In this he may seem admirably 'rational'. However, we must be sure that what is being stripped away really is illusion before we assent to such destructive rhetoric, as Roderigo quickly does. Iago demonstrates the scathing power of his mode of analysis by setting out to Roderigo the implausibility of Desdemona being anything other than briefly infatuated with Othello. The essence of what he says is that no one is capable of sticking to anything for very long. If Roderigo just waits his turn then his turn with her will come.

When he has won Roderigo over and Roderigo has left the stage, Iago returns to verse. In 22 efficient and sinewy lines he shows us more of himself than we have hitherto seen, and it is not a heartening sight. As soon as Roderigo has gone, Iago repudiates him, as though he wishes us to be clear that he is not spending time with such a 'snipe' for any other reason than his own advantage. It is often difficult to be sure to whom a soliloquy is being addressed, but these words are quite clearly spoken to an audience that Iago imagines he has. He takes a delight in showing us just how casually wicked he is. He is lightly but determinedly vindictive:

> I hate the Moor
> And it is thought abroad that 'twixt my sheets
> He's done my office. I know not if 't be true,

But I for mere suspicion in that kind
Will do as if for surety. (1.3.385–89)

We can take him at his word and then we have a man, stung by
rumours, eager to even the score, whether or not there is any truth
in the rumours. We can consider a more subtle psychology and
ask ourselves whether he might not be pretending, to himself as
much as to others, that he does not care whether there is any truth
in the rumours, but really he is deeply wounded and hurt to think
his wife unfaithful. Here we must ask what we prefer to believe
and why we prefer to believe it. Either picture can be maintained.

Act 2 sees him bandying coarse wit with Desdemona and then
bolstering Roderigo's resolve again. His determination to put the
worst construction upon the slightest of evidence quickly sways
the impressionable Roderigo. In Act 2, scene 3 he engineers the
downfall of Cassio and then in Act 3, scene 3 he sets about the
downfall of Othello. It all happens terribly quickly. He does it by
the simplest means:

IAGO: Ha, I like not that.
OTHELLO: What dost thou say?
IAGO: Nothing, my lord; or if – I know not what.
OTHELLO: Was not that Cassio parted from my wife?
IAGO: Cassio, my lord? no, sure, I cannot think it
That he would steal away so guilty-like
Seeing you coming. (3.3.34–39)

The important point is not whether his stratagem is well-founded
or not: what matters is that it works. Iago persuades Othello that
he is hiding something, and then gives a very good impression of
a man being forced very much against his will to reveal what he
is hiding.

It is Iago who introduces the word 'jealousy' (at line 167), but
it is vital to see that Othello does not recoil in surprise when it
emerges but groans 'O misery!' (at line 173). By the time Othello
has thought by himself for a little while, and Desdemona and
Emilia have happened by, and Emilia has given Iago the notori-
ous handkerchief, Iago can gloat:

> Look where he comes. Not poppy nor mandragora
> Nor all the drowsy syrups of the world
> Shall ever medicine thee to that sweet sleep
> Which thou owedst yesterday. (3.3.333–36)

It is important at this point to notice that Othello's disposition upon his return at line 332 is much worsened from what it was at his last soliloquy, already discussed, at lines 262–83. The last movement of that soliloquy is an anguished turn from almost infantile anger:

> I had rather be a toad
> And live upon the vapour of a dungeon
> Than keep a corner in the thing I love
> For others' uses. (3.3.274–277)

To:

> Look where she comes:
> If she be false, O then heaven mocks itself,
> I'll not believe't. (3.3.281–83)

At line 336 he says 'Ha! Ha! false to me?', and at line 341: 'What sense had I of her stolen hours of lust?' In other words, by this time he has become convinced not only that his wife *might* be unfaithful but that she *has* been, on many occasions. This is important because it is a reminder that, however clever Iago is, much of the work is done by Othello himself. This, in turn, is important if we are to avoid the trap into which Coleridge and Bradley and many others have fallen. If Othello is so noble, then how could he turn so nasty? Answer: because of the infernal guile of Iago. This makes Iago 'a being next to devil', in Coleridge's phrase, and though Coleridge is careful to continue: 'only *not* quite devil', this is a distinction that is hard to maintain. *Othello* is a tragedy because it is Othello's tragedy, if it is a tragedy at all; though it is also, certainly, to an extent, Desdemona's tragedy, and may be in part Iago's tragedy, it is not Iago's play and it is not Desdemona's play. Othello is the central character and however interesting Iago, or Desdemona, may be to us they should not be allowed to distract our attention from Othello or else the play becomes confusing and unbalanced.

After a point in this terrible scene, Iago begins to enjoy himself and to play with his captive. As Othello's fury grows and he demands proof, Iago almost cheekily asks him: 'Would you, the supervisor, grossly gape on? / Behold her topped?' (3.3.398–99). With breathtaking boldness Iago invites Othello to imagine Desdemona being 'topped', or penetrated, by Cassio as he asks Othello to consider what would constitute proof and, further, to agree with him that such proof would be difficult to secure. When Othello, in response, exclaims 'Death and damnation! O!', Iago continues to muse: 'It were a tedious difficulty, I think, / To bring them to that prospect' (3.3.399–401), thus further drawing out the picture he is painting of the imaginary encounter between Desdemona and Cassio. The scene ends with a hideous pact between the two. Othello falls to his knees at line 454: 'Now, by yond marble heaven / In the due reverence of a sacred vow / I here engage my words' (3.3.463–65), and at line 465 Iago kneels too:

> Witness, you ever-burning lights above,
> You elements that clip us round about,
> Witness that here Iago doth give up
> The execution of his wit, hands, heart
> To wronged Othello's service. Let him command
> And to obey shall be in me remorse
> What bloody business ever. (3.3.466–72)

The atmosphere evoked is given in the word 'reverence': this is a solemn, almost a ceremonial moment in which something irrevocable is enacted. The scene ends with a horrible parody of the promotion Iago wanted:

> OTHELLO: Now art thou my lieutenant.
> IAGO: I am your own for ever. (3.3.481–82)

The rest of the action to the murder sees Iago keeping the spinning top of his plot going. He appears now with Cassio, now with

Othello, now with Emilia and Desdemona, being to each of them what they expect him to be and he is, in one sense, not remarkable at all. As an experiment, let us try to imagine a world in which Iago is not the exception but the rule. What would such a world be like?

To find out, we need to return to the opening scenes, in which we learn so much about him. Right at the beginning, Iago puts his rhetorical skills on display. Roderigo has found out that Iago has been let in on the secret of Othello's engagement and marriage to Desdemona and Roderigo is incensed, feeling betrayed by the man whom he regarded as his friend and helped out with (we imagine) generous 'loans'. Iago wins him with a tale. This is to be a feature of this first part of the play. Othello tells the tale of his wooing of Desdemona with tales of his adventures; Iago here captures Roderigo's attention with a tale. He tells how his bid for promotion was thwarted when Othello appointed Cassio in his stead. Cassio is a 'great arithmetician' (1.1.18), 'That never set a squadron in the field / Nor the division of a battle knows / More than a spinster' (1.1.21–23), and so on. It is a good speech: it is forthright, downright, amusing. He draws the pompous Othello well and expresses his indignation colourfully. Roderigo is hooked, but retains enough self-possession to complain, 'I would not follow him then', which draws from Iago an interesting speech:

> O sir, content you!
> I follow him to serve my turn upon him.
> We cannot all be masters, nor all masters
> Cannot be truly followed. You shall mark
> Many a duteous and knee-crooking knave
> That, doting on his own obsequious bondage,
> Wears out his time much like his master's ass
> For nought but provender, and, when he's old, cashiered.
> Whip me such honest knaves! Others there are
> Who, trimmed in forms and visages of duty,
> Keep yet their hearts attending on themselves
> And, throwing but shows of service on their lords,
> Do well thrive by them, and when they have lined their coats,

Do themselves homage: these fellows have some soul
And such a one do I profess myself. (1.1.40–54)

It is always difficult to know how to approach such speeches. Edmund's soliloquy that opens Act 1, scene 2 of the *Tragedy of King Lear* is an example. Considered from a certain point of view, Edmund has a point: his being illegitimate is not his fault, nor is his being younger than his brother, and both conditions debar him from inheritance which, to some, may seem unfair. Iago reminds us that not all servants are rewarded, many are merely exploited. The question is, when a social order seems to be manifestly unfair, what is the proper attitude of the unfairly treated? A traditional Christian view is that suffering patiently endured is a conspicuous virtue; but another view might be that such a view is patently promoted in order to prolong an unjust order. If people who are exploited are suffering but believing that their suffering will be rewarded in heaven, how convenient is that for their exploiters? For Iago, these 'honest knaves' are contemptible. Those that have 'some soul' – and by 'soul' he means not 'virtue' in any traditional Christian sense but something like 'spirit' in the sense of 'energy' or 'vitality' – are those who pretend to be going along with things but are actually plotting against their exploiters. It is not difficult to see that such a person may see himself as a hero. After all, in occupied France during the Second World War, it was the Resistance who were the heroes, and not those who collaborated with the occupiers. Those who plotted in secret against the occupying army were not contemptible cheats but laudable heroes. William Empson (1951) says that it is easy to imagine that in a contemporary audience there would have been cashiered soldiers who would feel only that Iago was a decent fellow who understood the world the same way that they did.

Later, when he is expounding to Roderigo his version of what is love, if we recoil from his crudely reductive account are we merely falling for the romantic illusion that conceals what he is only being honest about, that it is 'merely a lust of the blood and a permission of the will' (1.3.335–6)? A world in which Iago were not exceptional, allowing for a certain degree of exaggeration in the characterization, would not be unlike our own world. We are sceptical about our political masters and suspicious of ideologies. In the famous phrase of Jean-François Lyotard, we display 'incredulity towards meta-narratives': we are more at home with small-scale accounts of our own and of other people's lives around us and less attracted to large-scale theories of national destiny or of world revolution. Lyotard's 'we', it must be said, refers to European intellectuals: but the tendency is quite widespread. Many people are more at home in micro-cultures and sub-cultures than they are in the macro-cultures of nations or even of regions, let alone groups of nations. In such a world, Othello's loyalty to Venice seems either calculating or naïve, and his romance with Desdemona incredible.

The next chapter will consider Iago and his place in the play, from the point of view of psychoanalytical theories prevalent in the mix of approaches that has characterized critical approaches to literature during the last quarter of the twentieth century and the beginning of the twenty-first century.

CHAPTER 5

IAGO: SIGN: FROM PSYCHOLOGY TO PSYCHOANALYSIS

We must remember that what we are doing as readers is deciphering the written characters on the page, which signify sounds, which signify, in turn, ideas. Some of these ideas are what we may call grammatical ideas: words such as 'the', 'and' and 'if'; words that connect other words to form phrases and sentences. Other words signify ideas that we may call 'substantive' ideas. These ideas are the ideas we have of the world of experience: of thought, and feeling, and judgement. The words we are reading here, the written characters, ultimately suggest to us the possible existence of a person who speaks these words, the kind of person who would speak these words. We construct this imaginary person and we are able to do this because we are following certain clues: we have certain expectations that lead us to draw certain conclusions. That's how writing works – and it is writing we are dealing with now, although this is writing to be turned into acting, into theatre.

The character of Iago may owe something to the medieval dramatic tradition of depicting particular aspects of character, such as Vice, as characters themselves. If we consider plays such as the anonymously-authored *Everyman* that belongs to the end of the fifteenth century, then we see that the drama is the interplay between personifications of ideas: it is allegorical in form. We can trace the development of the dramatization of individual personalities in the history of the drama and see Renaissance drama as the full flowering of this developed interest in persons. On the other hand we may argue that the allegorical tendency – the tendency to symbolize – did not go away but lies buried, as it were, beneath the surface of the developed interest in persons. We may say that the developed interest in persons distracted us from the main structure of drama and made us think that what we were watching should resemble everyday life more than perhaps it can or should.

F. R. Leavis (1937) thought that A. C. Bradley (1991) and Coleridge (1969) had gone too far in the direction of discussing plays as though they were real life, and that this had distorted their impression of what works of art can do and should be doing. Art may resemble life but it is not life: and in that distinction lies all the value of art. Leavis takes issue with the 'Bradley-Coleridge' Othello, as we have already seen, and argues that they must also distort Iago if they are to maintain their view of Othello, making Iago an unnaturally over-developed dramatic figure commanding an interest quite out of proportion to his place in the play, when that is properly understood. Leavis argues that Iago is a dramatic mechanism:

> Considered as a comprehensibly villainous person, he represents a not uncommon kind of grudging, cynical malice (and he's given, at least in suggestion, enough in the way of grievance and motive). But in order to perform his function as dramatic machinery he has to put on such an appearance of invincibly cunning devilry as to provide Coleridge and the rest with some excuse for their awe, and to leave others wondering, in critical reflection, whether he isn't a rather clumsy mechanism. (Leavis 1937, 278)

Jan Kott agreed that:

> The demonic Iago was an invention of the romantics. Iago is no demon. Like Richard III, he is a contemporary careerist, but on a different scale. (Kott 1967, 86)

William Empson's brilliant essay, 'Honest in *Othello*', discusses Iago in terms of changing meanings of the word 'evil':

> There seems a linguistic difference between what Shakespeare meant by Iago and what the nineteenth century critics saw in him. They took him as an abstract term 'Evil'; he is a critique on an unconscious pun. This is seen more clearly in their own

personifications of their abstract word; e.g. *The Turn of the Screw* and *Dr Jekyll and Mr Hyde*. Henry James got a great triumph over some critic who said that his villains were sexual perverts (if the story meant anything they could hardly be anything else). He said: 'Ah, you have been letting yourself have fancies about Evil; I kept it right out of my mind.' That indeed is what the story is about. Stevenson rightly made clear that *Dr Jekyll* is about hypocrisy. You can only consider Evil as all things that destroy the good life; this has no unity; for instance, Hyde could not be both the miser and the spendthrift and whichever he was would destroy Jekyll without further accident. Evil here is merely the daydream of a respectable man, and only left vague so that respectable readers may equate it unshocked to their own daydreams. Iago may not be a 'personality', but he is better than these; he is the product of a more actual interest in a word (Empson 1951, 230–1).

The fascinating suggestion here is that plays (and stories and novels) 'personify' (i.e. put into concrete action) abstractions such as notions of 'evil'. Comparing these 'personifications' will give us insights into changing outlooks over time. The nineteenth century 'meant' something, that is, *understood* something, differently when it thought about evil from what Shakespeare at least, and some others in his time perhaps, thought when they brought the idea to mind and clothed it in character and action.

Thomas Rymer had famously argued that Iago is so untypical that we can learn nothing from him:

Shakespear knew his Character of *Jago* was inconsistent. In this very Play he pronounces,
   If thou dost deliver more or less than Truth,
   Thou are no Souldier. (2.3.215–16)
This he knew, but to entertain the Audience with something new and surprising, against common sense, and Nature, he would pass upon us a close, dissembling, false, insinuating rascal, instead of an open-hearted, frank, plain-dealing Souldier, a character constantly worn by them for some thousands of years in the World. (Rymer 1956, 134–5).

Rymer distinguished, after Aristotle, between History and Philosophy, and claimed that Iago is a piece of history, not of philosophy, and therefore can't mean anything:

> *Philosophy* tells us it is a principle in the Nature of Man *to be grateful*. *History* may tell us that *John an Oaks, John a Stiles*, or *Jago* were ungrateful; *Poetry* is to follow Nature: Philosophy must be his guide: history and *fact* in particular cases of *John an Oaks*, or *John of Styles*, are no warrant or direction for a Poet. Therefore *Aristotle* is always telling us that Poetry is [. . .] more general and abstracted, is led more by the Philosophy, the reason and nature of things, than History: which only records things higlety, piglety, right or wrong as they happen. History might without any preamble or difficulty, say that *Jago* was ungrateful. Philosophy then calls him unnatural. (Rymer 1956, 163)

In other words, what may happen in the real world is not what poetry should address; poetry should address an ideal world imagined by philosophy. This is like saying that everything in art should be (and is) *representative*; that is, that though things are in art as they appear, they are also representative of classes of things (so Othello represents, or stands for, soldiers, 'Moors', men; Desdemona represents, or stands for, women, young people, aristocrats; and so on). The more individual a character is in a play, the less he or she can represent. The less they can represent, the less we can learn from them.

If we look at this from another point of view, however, we see that we are learning about human possibility from the delineation of individual character. If it is possible for us to imagine someone doing something, then it is humanly possible that it be done: we may believe that we *should* never do it, but we may reflect that we shall need to be very confident about the solidity of 'character' to be sure that we, or those we know, *could* never do it.

At this point a diversion on what has come to be called 'Critical Theory' or 'theory' is useful. We have already encountered this in looking at Valerie Traub's discussion of *Othello*: Traub, it should be stressed, is not attempting to show that Shakespeare intended these meanings – she is showing what the text may be led to mean. This unconcern with 'intention' marks much twentieth-century criticism. The identification of the 'Intentional Fallacy' by two American critics, W. K. Wimsatt and Monroe C. Beardsley (1946), steered critical interest away from the attempt to demonstrate what the author meant because, as Wimsatt and Beardsley argued so effectively, what the author meant is irrecoverable and anyway irrelevant. What mattered was what the text meant. We may speak as though we were uncovering the author's intention, as long as we realize that in most cases we cannot anyway, as the author is deceased, and that even if we could it would not be of any importance. This should remind us that such bad habits (if they are) such as treating characters as though they were people are very hard to lose.

Critical theory embraces a not altogether harmonious collection of approaches, sharing both an aggressive version of the hostility to such bad habits that characterizes much twentieth-century criticism, and a determination to look beyond what the text appears to mean and to further realities, which more intense critical attention may uncover. The relationship between critical theory and other forms of criticism may be caricatured by suggesting that where other forms of critical practice take the text to mean what its says, critical theory holds that it cannot mean what it says.

Sigmund Freud gives an account in *The Interpretation of Dreams* that is of relevance here, of a dream told to him by a patient who was delighted with the dream until Freud interpreted it for her. He notes with some smugness that she 'lost her liking for this pretty dream after it had been interpreted' (Freud 1954, 347). Marxist accounts of texts drawing on notions of 'ideology' often take a similar form: the passage or the text may appear to mean one thing but can be made, upon analysis from a certain point of view, to mean another. This sort of approach is often called 'cultural materialism' and is a British cousin to New Historicism in the USA. What both approaches have fastened on is that such matters as what human nature is (or the nature of 'man' and 'woman') are not fixed, but vary according to the historical circumstances in which the discussion is taking place, and that it is the duty of the critic above all to mark the *differences*, and not to collude with a process of assimilation by which differences are either subsumed into dominant versions of what is human or natural, or denied human or natural status altogether. This is obviously central to the discussion between Iago and Othello in Act 3, scene 3 in which Iago gets Othello to reflect: 'And yet how nature, erring from itself' (3.3.231). At this point he is making a crucial mistake: how can nature 'err from itself'? For it to do that it must remain nature (doing the 'erring') and yet be other than itself ('erring from itself'). It cannot be both at the same time. Nevertheless we know what he means: a person may incline away from what is human nature; someone may do or want something 'unnatural'. However, we may only 'know' that this is what he means if we are prepared to interpret what he says. We must go beyond what his words appear to mean and postulate a meaning that makes sense, and then further postulate that it is that meaning he really intended. We can go further, however, if we recall that the ideas that bind a society together may indeed be self-contradictory.

If we look at what he says, then it is contradictory, but perhaps that is because there is no 'natural' and no 'unnatural' and no 'human nature', either except in ideology, in socially constructed imaginings which, when tested, prove to be inadequate. Othello cannot mean what he wants to mean because it is contradictory: wants and desires are as much a part of 'nature' as anything else. If you want to say that something someone wants is 'unnatural', then you must be able to say how it is that they want it. If they want it because they themselves are 'unnatural' then they cannot be human beings because they are not 'natural'. In this way people perceived as 'other' may be demonized by those perceiving them, such as colonists encountering a native population. This is where critical theory comes in.

A Marxist account will want to take class as a determinant in its analysis, and it will take class as itself determined by positioning in the economic and political structures of society at any time. A classic Marxist account of *Othello* would look at the class structure of Venetian society as it is shown to us in the play, and point out that Venice is a mercantile society, a 'bourgeois' society, based on the accumulation of capital and not on the acquisition of or tenure of land and its cultivation; that its characteristic features will therefore be political liberalism and social mobility, compared with aristocratic society's tendency towards rigid hierarchies and positions determined by inheritance; and that its culture will be marked by individualism rather than fixed sets of values. Aristocracy is, at the point of origin, military in character, but bourgeois society, though quite ready to wage war, does not locate social power in military terms so much as in economic advantage: Othello's rather old-fashioned, 'chivalric', outlook, romanticizing war and soldiery, belongs to an aristocratic form of society, and so in this he is again something of an outsider. Iago, in such a view, can seem to be almost a revolutionary spirit, seeing through the pretences of the world in which he lives and acting with a determined consistency to expose and destroy those pretences.

Unfortunately, such high principles sit very uneasily with the character as we can construct him from the play. This is a good example of interpretation exceeding its authority. What we can say is that bourgeois society, at a certain point in its development, exhausts the stock of belief with which it invested itself at its beginnings, and by its persistent failure to live up to its ideals encourages a wholly destructive cynical unbelief in some of those it fails to reward (or who feel that they should have been rewarded more than they have been). It is bourgeois society's incapacity to erect and live up to a convincing morality that is its cultural downfall. However, Marxists schooled in Leninism would want to point out that such disbelief may corrode but can never overthrow bourgeois society: only the organized working class, led by a political party shaped by the discipline of correctly worked-out theoretical positions, can achieve this overthrow of bourgeois society and the establishment of first a socialist and, finally, a communist society.

Alternatively, political analyses may point out how accounts such as Coleridge's and A. C. Bradley's have the effect of glamourizing the military ideals and hence the aristocratic principles that the play might be seen to enshrine in Othello himself, and the demonizing of Iago might then seem to be the attempt to warn us away from the evils of discontent and dissent from the established order. Critics influenced by Marxist ideas, such as Jonathan Dollimore (1985) or Graham Holderness (1985), have often pointed out that the History plays may be read as justifications of the Elizabethan political settlement: *Othello* may be read as a justification of a liberal oligarchy such as that which the London merchants had established among themselves, and an idealization of a commercial polity such as Venice in fact was and as many Londoners, and others, hoped that England might become. The balanced, sympathetic, principled figures, though minor characters – Lodovico and Montano, and the Duke himself – may be seen to be representative of the fundamental good sense of this kind of society, and Iago as its characteristic dissenter, dangerous only to the innocent idealist and dealt with firmly by the wise state.

Valerie Traub's essay, discussed in the second chapter, shows us what a feminist account looks like. Feminists take gender as analytically determinant and by gender they mean not biological sex but socially-determined gender – we may say, not male and female but masculine and feminine. Human characteristics are organized under the headings 'masculine' or 'feminine', that is, as properly belonging to men or properly belonging to women. These characteristics are not the exclusive property of men or of women: men may show feminine characteristics and women may show masculine characteristics. The question is, what are men supposed to be like and what are women supposed to be like?

In *Othello* the burden of such a discussion would fall on Othello and Desdemona, but Iago has his place in the debate. Particularly in his persistent debasing of sexual activity, Iago stresses sexual appetite as a determinant and insistently describes Desdemona as a creature of sexual appetite. It is sometimes said that gender-based ideologies tend to see women as either virgins or whores: Iago sees women as whores.

When he and Roderigo are shouting outside Brabantio's window, it is Iago who keeps bringing the banter back to a distinctly, and aggressively, sexual content:

Even now, now, very now, an old black ram
Is tupping your white ewe! (1.1.87–88)

Here, Iago, with impressive economy, blends three grounds of prejudice – race, age and gender – in one insulting and degrading comparison of Othello and Desdemona to 'an old black ram' and a 'white ewe'. In a few lines he will warn Brabantio that his dithering will result in his having his 'daughter covered with a Barbary [Arabian] horse' (1.1.110), and later again he warns Brabantio that 'your daughter and the Moor are now making the beast with two backs' (1.1.114–15), referring to a traditional description of a couple engaged in sexual intercourse. At the end of Act 1 he paints a picture for Roderigo of 'love' that is utterly reductive:

> If the balance of our lives had not one scale of reason to poise another of sensuality, the blood and baseness of our natures would conduct us to most preposterous conclusions. But we have reason to cool our raging motions, our carnal stings, our unbitted lusts; whereof I take this, that you call love, to be a sect or scion. (1.3.327–33)

In such speeches Iago may be thought of as a Critical Theorist himself, of a sort. He has seen through, in his view at least, all the pretences of his society and has satisfied himself that there is no truth to human being but lust and greed. Women are every bit as bad as men – appetite is all: 'She must change for youth; when she is sated with his body she will find the error of her choice' (1.3.350–52). He returns to this theme in Cyprus. Exchanging jests with Desdemona on the quayside, he challenges her:

> Come on, come on, you are pictures out of doors,
> Bells in your parlours, wild-cats in your kitchens,
> Saints in your injuries, devils being offended,
> Players in your housewifery, and housewives in . . .
> Your beds! (2.1.109–13)

Desdemona replies: 'O, fie upon thee, slanderer!' (2.1.113), and he comes back: 'Nay it is true, or else I am a Turk: / You rise to play, and go to bed to work' (2.1.114–15). This is a common theme of popular caricatures of sexual relationships as power struggles, but placed in amongst Iago's habitual reflections it has a darker side.

A psychoanalytical account is, like a more traditional psychological–moral account, an account of the psychology of the characters, but applying to the characters the ideas developed by Sigmund Freud and (rather more rarely) Carl Gustav Jung. Freud himself famously claimed to derive some of his ideas from an observation of Shakespeare's work, and this suggests an important reflection: that such applications of Freud's theories to Shakespeare's works are less a way of opening them up to a scrutiny they could not perform on themselves than they are a compliment to Shakespeare's sagacity, and the truth of his depictions of human being.

A much more controversial development of Freudian theory (which took predominantly as its object the analysis of patients) has been undertaken in recent years, towards analysis of discourse itself. Here, psychoanalysis and linguistics join forces (in the work of Jacques Lacan and Émile Benveniste, for example) to probe what might be thought of as a 'common mind' or the 'mind' of a culture. If we think of culture as necessarily being interaction then we may think of the individual mind much less as an 'atom', as it were, than as a point in a set of intersecting lines of interaction; and then we can think of culture as itself a 'mind' of a sort. The point can be illustrated by thinking about language itself.

Language was learned by each of us. We are inducted into a set of terms, relationships, categories, ideas, concepts and feelings that we come to call our own because we are continually checking our own experience as individual human beings against the language we are learning, and gauging the likeness and unlikeness of our experience and the common experience enshrined in language. Of course, as we are using language to do this we are bringing our 'own' experience more and more into line with that segment of the common experience with which we are most familiar. It is, then, possible to imagine culture as a continuous texture, as it were, into which each of us is woven, and which is woven throughout our own being as well, so that it is not possible to determine exactly where one ends and the other begins:

what is 'me' and what is 'my culture'. Thus a psychoanalytical approach is permitted to pass beyond the immediate brief, the analysis of the individual subject, out to analysis of the culture as a whole. The relevance of these ideas to *Othello* is obvious, as the subject of the play is sexual jealousy and though sexual jealousy is, from one point of view, an individual's experience, the relationships within which such emotions arise are unmistakably social. Thus the audience, and the reader, is plunged immediately into the social world of the tensions that belong to sexual desire.

Iago is as compelling from this point of view as is Othello himself for, in both cases, there is a serious uncertainty about their motives. Othello's speech upon entering Desdemona's bedchamber at the beginning of Act 5, scene 2 is an extraordinarily slippery piece of work:

It is the cause, it is the cause, my soul!
Let me not name it to you, you chaste stars,
It is the cause. Yet I'll not shed her blood
Nor scar that whiter skin of hers than snow
And smooth as monumental alabaster:
Yet she must die, else she'll betray more men.
Put out the light, and then put out the light!
If I quench thee, thou flaming minister,
I can again thy former light restore
Should I repent me. But once put out thy light,
Thou cunning'st pattern of excelling nature,
I know not where is that Promethean heat
That can thy light relume: when I have plucked the rose
I cannot give it vital growth again,
It needs must wither. I'll smell thee on the tree;
O balmy breath, that dost almost persuade
Justice to break her sword! Once more, once more:
Be thus when thou art dead and I will kill thee
And love thee after. Once more, and that's the last.
                              He [smells then] kisses her
So sweet was ne'er so fatal. I must weep,
But they are cruel tears. This sorrow's heavenly,
It strikes where it doth love. She wakes. (5.2.1–22)

The overall pattern of this speech displays three key features: the rhythms of desire; an apparent reluctance to do what he has come to do; and a systematic symbolism over which Othello has no control. These three are connected. We should be in no doubt that Othello has come to murder Desdemona, and that he is doing so because he hates her, and that he hates her because she has made him madly jealous. What he is doing here is trying to cope with the pressure of unconscious material against the structures that hold his conscious being together. Othello is a warrior who lives by a code of justice: he is a guardian. This is how he sees himself, and he is proud of himself as living this role effectively. That much we have seen. At this point, however, he is doing as he likes, driven by unconscious promptings that have come dangerously close to the surface as he has begun to lose conscious control.

The 'ego', as it is called in the English translation from Freud's original German, finds itself under attack from the inchoate, powerful desires of the 'id', the earliest, uncontrolled wishes of infancy against the power of which the 'ego' has been formed as a defence mechanism. The ego has grounded itself in acts of repression and disavowal that have created distance from these early forces, pretending desperately that they are not the wishes of the conscious self and trying, almost hopelessly, to forget about them, as though wishing them away might relieve the poor ego of their pressure upon it. Here we see Othello's fragile ego, worn by the pressures under which it has been put, giving way fitfully, revealing the savage and tormented world of the id.

The confusion begins with the opening phrase: 'It' has no antecedent. We listen in puzzlement to someone preoccupied with something he does not, or cannot, or will not, identify. If we accept for a moment that he will not identify his preoccupation then we can further suggest that this unwillingness might imply an obsession with something the speaker must hold at arm's length or else be threatened by. Freud's *Three Essays on the Theory of Sexuality* develop a fascinating discussion of fetishism, in which he describes it as a process of deferral by means of which the fetishist symbolizes something to which he is drawn, and from which he is simultaneously repelled: the revelation (which is in fact a repressed knowledge) that the woman does not possess a penis (Freud, 1962). The symbol both brings nearer (because it refers to) and puts off (because it is not) the desired and feared object, female genitalia. Othello's fumbling at the beginning of Act 5, scene 2 might suggest this dreadful ambivalence. He refers to 'it' without defining 'it' because he desires 'it' and fears 'it'. 'It' only becomes clear when he says 'Yet I'll not shed her blood / Nor scar that whiter skin of hers than snow / And smooth as monumental alabaster' (5.2.3–5). Now we see (or we can interpret these phrases as meaning) that her sexual attractiveness to him is what he feels he must destroy.

The shape of the entire speech is disturbed by a mixture of preoccupied intensity and a desultory irrelevance that looks like a disturbance of mind. He jumps from one idea to another, as he does when he suddenly collects himself: 'Yet she must die, else she'll betray more men' (5.2.6). He moves from serious considerations to trivial and he makes puns (as he does when he says 'Put out the light, and then put out the light!'), and pursues odd, paradoxical connections and contrasts, as he does in the almost fugal musings that follow from 'Put out the light'.

With this clue we can go further and suggest that the sexual symbolism is not his, in the sense that it is not consciously controlled, but emerges at the urging of a deeper, unconscious set of promptings: the sword of justice becomes the erect penis, the *phallus*; the 'rose' is Desdemona's virginity, or her genitalia; Desdemona herself is fetishized into her components ('blood' and 'skin'); Othello imagines her as a statue ('As smooth as monumental alabaster'); he imagines possessing her corpse: 'Be thus when thou art dead and I will kill thee / And love thee after' (5.2.18–19).

We have seen earlier warning signs:

> I had rather be a toad
> And live upon the vapour of a dungeon
> Than keep a corner in the thing I love
> For others' uses. (3.3.274–77)

This comes after a passage of measured reflection, sad resignation and generous goodwill towards her, which is followed by wistful and perhaps slightly self-pitying speculation on the reasons for the loss of her love. Then he bursts out: 'O curse of marriage / That we can call these delicate creatures ours / And not their appetites!' (3.3.272–74), and then – all the more surprising for a man whose habitual imagery is grand, if not grandiose – he compares himself with a toad in a dungeon in an image of angry self-deprecation and infantile rage that a possession of his has been spoiled for him by 'others' uses'. Later, in Act 4, scene 1, there comes this:

> Lie with her? Lie on her? We say lie on her when they belie her! Lie with her, zounds, that's fulsome! – Handkerchief! confessions! handkerchief! – To confess, and be hanged for his labour! First to be hanged, and then to confess: I tremble at it. Nature would not invest herself in such shadowing passion without some instruction. It is not words that shakes me thus. Pish! Noses, ears, and lips. Is't possible? Confess! Handkerchief! O devil!
>
> [*He*] *falls in a trance* (4.1.35–43)

He recovers enough to bait Desdemona terribly in Act 4, scene 2 but not before he has struck her in public and parted from Lodovico with the extraordinary: 'You are welcome, sir, to Cyprus. Goats and monkeys!' (4.1.263). These words pick up Iago's taunting him earlier: 'Would you, the supervisor, grossly gape on? / Behold her topped?' (3.3.398–99). Iago continues:

> It is impossible you should see this
> Were they as prime as goats, as hot as monkeys,
> As salt as wolves in pride, and fools as gross
> As ignorance made drunk. (3.3.405–08)

Othello has not forgotten these words. His outbursts show the fissure in his mind: the bursting out of unconscious material as his self-control is weakened, and as the ego gives way before the force of the id. The next chapter will take this form of analysis further into a closer look at Iago and will then turn away from the inner life towards the outer, towards history – but not at the expense of psychoanalytical perspectives. Integrating, through the figure of discourse, inner and outer (and abolishing, we may say, the distinction between the two realms, and perhaps with the distinction the realms themselves), we enter a new world for critical reflection to inhabit and to explore.

CHAPTER 6

IAGO: SIGN: FROM PSYCHE TO CLIO

The Greek word *psyche* was used to indicate the soul or spirit, but it also meant a butterfly, and was the name of the girl visited nightly by a mysterious lover she was warned never to try to look upon. She lost him for ever, upon yielding to a terrible curiosity and setting a trap to reveal his identity, at the very moment he was found to be the god Cupid. Such delicate and elusive meanings are appropriate for the complexes of the imagination painstakingly mapped out by Freud and his followers (although there are other traditions, such as Jungian 'depth psychology', it is Freudian psychoanalysis that has attracted literary critics); but this inner life has often been contrasted vigorously by the outer life – the life of public affairs, of History. The Greeks named Clio the daughter of Zeus responsible for inspiring the historian, and for many writers Psyche and Clio have seemed to be opposing influences. Marx was not much interested in the inner life, believing that it was in the social structures into which men were inescapably precipitated at birth that determined behaviour, and not whatever went on inside in the mean time. One of the achievements of Critical Theory in the late twentieth century has been the engagement of psychoanalytical with Marxist perspectives to offer new ways of looking at and thinking about cultural activity.

Reflection along psychoanalytical lines will lead us to conclude that Shakespeare's interest is in the pathology of sexual jealousy, not only as it is manifested in Othello, at which we have already glanced, but also as it is manifested in Iago. This may seem to be an odd view, as all commentators on Iago point out that he tells us himself that his motive is his irritation at being passed over for promotion: however, at two points Iago makes clear what we might as well regard as his real motive, not forgetting that the more widely accepted motive is that which he gave Roderigo, while these passages given here are from his addresses to us as his private audience:

> I hate the Moor
> And it is thought abroad that 'twixt my sheets
> He's done my office. I know not if't be true,
> But I for mere suspicion in that kind,
> Will do as if for surety. (1.3.385–89)

And again:

> That Cassio loves her, I do well believe it,
> That she loves him, 'tis apt and of great credit.
> The Moor, howbeit that I endure him not,
> Is of a constant, loving, noble nature,
> And I dare think he'll prove to Desdemona
> A most dear husband. Now I do love her too,
> Not out of absolute lust – though peradventure
> I stand accountant for as great a sin –
> But partly led to diet my revenge,
> For that I do suspect the lusty Moor
> Hath leaped into my seat, the thought whereof
> Doth like a poisonous mineral gnaw my inwards . . .
> And nothing can or shall content my soul
> Till I am evened with him, wife for wife . . . (2.1.284–97)

The common view of the play's action is given fairly by Rymer:

> Othello, a Blackmoor Captain, by talking of his Prowess and Feats of War, makes Desdemona a Senator's Daughter to be in love with him; and to be married to him, without her Parents' knowledge; And having preferred Cassio, to be his Lieutenant, (a place which his Ensign Jago sued for) Jago in revenge, works the Moor into a Jealousy that Cassio Cuckolds him: which he

effects by stealing and conveying a certain Handkerchief, which had, at the Wedding, been by the Moor presented to his Bride. Hereupon, Othello and Jago plot the deaths of Desdemona and Cassio, Othello Murders her, and soon after is convinced of her Innocence. And as he is about to be carried to Prison, in order to be punish'd for the Murder, He kills himself. (Rymer 1956, 132)

In fact the reason for Iago's hatred of Othello is not his being passed over for promotion, but his jealous suspicions of his wife Emilia's conduct. His hating Othello because he preferred Cassio is the reason Iago gives Roderigo; and his use of the word 'love' is fascinating if we pursue our psychoanalytically-influenced investigations.

Iago has defined love for us in his conversation with Roderigo, discussed earlier, towards the end of Act 1:

IAGO: If the balance of our lives had not one scale of reason to poise another of sensuality, the blood and baseness of our natures would conduct us to most preposterous conclusions. But we have reason to cool our raging motions, our carnal stings, our unbitted lusts; whereof I take this, that you call love, to be a sect or scion.
RODERIGO: It cannot be.
IAGO: It is merely a lust of the blood and a permission of the will. (1.3.326–36)

The point has been made in the previous chapter that we should think carefully about what Iago means by 'reason': he means a calculating awareness of the odds; a self-interested cleverness. In the same way, what he means by 'love' means here 'merely a lust of the blood and a permission of the will'. In *The Innocence of Dreams*, Charles Rycroft discusses the 'most preposterous conclusions' which we enact, in his view, in dreams, to which the will unbalanced by reason (in Iago's model) would lead us in waking life (Rycroft, 1981). It is not irrelevant to note that Thomas Hobbes's famous essay *Leviathan* (1651) takes a not dissimilar view, proposing that society imposes the necessity of such control and that it is accepted because our reasoned view is that it is better to have some of what we want than to risk not having any, as Hobbes maintains we otherwise would in the natural state (Hobbes, 1998). This is not to malign Hobbes: it is to contextualize Iago. A comparison with Edmund's bold individualism in *King Lear* (and tendencies to rationalize away the restraints of custom and law) is an equally useful contribution to an attempt to situate Iago in his time, the early seventeenth century, the eve of religious and political revolution and civil war. This will lead us towards New Historicism, to which we will return.

Iago offers in Act 2 a further distinction: he 'loves' Desdemona, 'not out of absolute lust' (2.1.290). This fastidiousness has the simultaneously fascinating and repellent quality of the fastidious discrimination of the Marquis de Sade, for whom sexual activity would seem to have no charm were it not harmful, illegal or sacrilegious or, perhaps preferably, all three. Iago feels the need to discriminate his feeling for Desdemona from 'absolute lust' and, to revert for a moment to the more traditional psychologizing of the previous chapter, we may speculate that this is because he does not want to be enslaved by anything, including powerful feeling. This is the sophisticated amateur position: he can take it or leave it. This makes Desdemona a figure of desire in a way in which her character will be explored in the next chapter: what we must note at this point is that Iago entertains himself with his own careful fastidiousness before reverting, and notably with much less self-control, to his theme of jealous fury. In this it is striking to what extent he anticipates the figure Othello will come to cut as Iago's ministrations have their effect: 'the thought whereof / Doth like a poisonous mineral gnaw my inwards' (2.1.294–95). From Act 3, scene 3 onwards Othello has not one moment's peace from this inward gnawing, and we may reflect that Iago has been similarly troubled, but for much longer. Emilia comes perilously close to the truth in Act 4, scene 2, guessing, with brilliant intuition, that:

> Some eternal villain,
> Some busy and insinuating rogue,

Some cogging, cozening slave, to get some office,
[Has] devised this slander. (4.2.132–35)

And later she adds:

Some such squire he was
That turned your wit the seamy side without
And made you to suspect me with the Moor. (4.2.147–49)

From a psychoanalytical point of view, jealousy is not engendered by suspicion, however reasonable or unreasonable, but by
desire. It is the reflex of desire. As desire is desire to possess
wholly, jealousy is the anxious doubt of possession. Because
desire wants something unreasonable and unattainable, so is the
anxiety more acute that it cannot be attained; and so the fantasy
of the possibility of its attainment by another (the unkindest cut
of all) forms increasingly a dread in the desirer's soul and gnaws
his inwards. The unreasonableness of desire is beautifully caught
by W. B. Yeats in 'The Man who Dreamed of Faeryland' (1893)
'His heart hung all upon a silken dress.' The metonymic nature
of desire; its resolution always in proximate and temporary conditions; its fleeting nature; its essential instability: all these are
expressed in the perception that it is surely the wearer of the dress
that is the object of desire, and the subsequent realization that it
is strictly speaking neither dress nor wearer but the dress worn
that is desired. Fetishism suddenly seems entirely reasonable. Its
expression in the form of jealousy in *Othello* is unmistakable: the
genius of the device of the handkerchief is that such a 'trifle' (as
both Iago and Emilia call it) can have such a profound effect.
Othello rightly talks of 'magic in the web' (3.4.71); Emilia says
that Desdemona 'so loves the token [. . .] That she reserves it
evermore about her / To kiss and talk to' (3.3.297–300). Iago too
is interested in the handkerchief long before he finds a specific
use for it:

that handkerchief thou speak'st of
I found by fortune and did give my husband,
For often, with a solemn earnestness

– More than indeed belonged to such a trifle –
He begged of me to steal't. (5.2.223–37)

It is a persuasive interpretation of that fascinating 'with a solemn earnestness / – More than indeed belonged to such a trifle' that it expresses a powerful, fetishistic obsession. The power of a symbol is manifested for us here in the poetry of the play, and we may easily talk of the power of the fetish.

We can add to this account an undercurrent of homoeroticism. It is not only Iago's dream that suggests the theme but, more importantly, the sinister mutual dedication of Iago and Othello, ritualized in their kneeling together at the end of Act 3. When Othello says 'Now art thou my lieutenant' (3.3.481), and Iago replies 'I am your own for ever' (3.3.482), it is not merely fanciful (and it works well in performance) for Iago to look longingly at Othello. Then the audience may suspect that repressed homosexual desire in Iago fuels his rage, his antagonism towards Emilia, his 'love' for Desdemona, and his contemptuously sceptical attitude towards the conduct of sexual relationships. The peculiar silence at the end of the play on his part, 'Demand me nothing. What you know, you know. / From this time forth I never will speak word' (5.2.300–1), may be explained (again, not entirely fancifully) as the silence of satisfied desire, and the murder as the enactment by symbolism of that act Iago longs for but cannot acknowledge, even – or perhaps especially – to himself.

Finally, we may add his attitude to Cassio. There is his afterthought interjected at 2.1.305, 'For I fear Cassio with my nightcap, too'; and much later at 5.1.19–20, when he is deliberating with himself whether Cassio should be killed or not, he says 'He hath a daily beauty in his life / That makes me ugly.' Iago's envious rage cannot be easily accounted for unless we reach into the sorts of interpretation offered by psychoanalysis, any more than Othello's jealous rage can be. Though envy and jealousy are distinct (there is always a third person in jealousy), they are not in Iago himself, who moves easily between the two and even confuses them, as he does, perhaps, with respect to Cassio: we learn that a definite rumour was spread regarding Emilia and Othello, but Cassio's interest in Emilia is Iago's own invention.

The great weakness of psychoanalytical accounts of literary or dramatic texts is that in the psychoanalytical encounter itself, the analysand ('the patient') is brought to acknowledge the rightness of the analysis: who is the analysand in this case? We must say that any psychoanalytical account of this play (or of any other) is only provisional: there is no analysand whose acknowledge-ment of the truth of the interpretation is a step on the road to healing. There are only characters dreamed up by the writer, the actors, the audience, the reader, which may as well be indicators of the psychic condition of those collaborators as they are indi-cators of anything else. The play may be a mirror in which we are seeing ourselves, in other words. That will have its uses, of course. We may well learn from the experience (though Thomas Rymer for one will say that what we learn we are better off not thinking about). Can we go any further?

If Benveniste and others are right then we may. 'Discourse' will allow us to say something about the collective mind, as it were, of the age that produced the work and about our consumption of it (which is a form of production, as we make it anew each time we read or perform or watch it). If we have a theory of history, then we may distinguish between the age in which it was first produced and the age in which we are now considering it: and that is what New Historicism does. Characteristically, New Historicist approaches take a document or documents from the age in which the work was produced and, by careful comparison, bring out the distinctive qualities of the age and, by implication or by direct analysis, the distinctiveness of that age in compari-son with our own. At points this comes to suggest that the past is unintelligible to the present, not just in fact but in principle. The implication and sometimes the direct statement is that the present cannot know the past and can therefore only know itself, and even that will only ever be an incomplete knowledge.

What are the implications of this position for criticism? In one respect New Historicism is very like traditional Historicism in the assertion that the past can only be reconstructed, interrogated and discussed in itself; and so New Historicist critical accounts of the play tend to look more like history than they look like criticism. This is a useful corrective, though, to the idea we may have (perhaps without thinking about it) that the plays are somehow free from history and 'true' at all points in space and time, at all points in geography and history. So the play performed in nineteenth-century Russia is the play performed in early twenty-first-century Indonesia, for example. Put this way the idea seems positively absurd: of course in either of those situations there may be points at which what is going on is recognizable, but there will also be points at which some research and scholarship will have to be done by or on behalf of the audiences and readers so that the differences between their lives and the lives created by the play will not be only baffling. In fact the same is true for most early twenty-first-century (and, for that matter, most twentieth-century, early, middle or late) readings and watchings of the play: there are significant differences between us and the lives created by the play on stage or in the mind's eye of the reader, and those differences cannot simply be wished away. Of course the points of recognition must outnumber or otherwise appear to us to be more significant than the points of misrecognition or non-recognition, or we should not be bothering with the work except as a part of history: but that knowledge must not lead us to ignore the differences.

What 'discourses' may we recognize in *Othello*? I should like to suggest that there are four that we should concentrate on: race; sexuality; politics; and religion. By 'race' I mean 'kind' more generally than we usually use the term currently: I mean to indicate what Iago indicates when he says 'I know our country disposition well' (3.3.204). Othello is an outsider not only because he is a 'Moor' but also because he is not a Venetian. When Brabantio utters to Iago and Roderigo the riposte 'What tell'st thou me of robbing? This is Venice: / My house is not a grange' (1.1.104–05), he is appealing to cosmopolitanism against the isolatedness of the country and is, implicitly, contrasting the 'largeness' of the town to the 'smallness' of the village. The irony here is that the town of which he is so proud is, in the wider world, a village. This leads into politics: Brabantio is a senator, a member of the ruling oligarchy of Venice, which is a republic; the Duke is not a monarch but a *primus inter pares* ('first among equals'). Venice is at war with the Ottoman Turkish Empire; this brings in religion, as the Ottoman Empire is Islamic and Venice is Christian.

The idea of discourse does not address so much explicit discourses, such as politics and religion – that is, consciously organized accounts such as essays, treatises and debates: it is much more concerned with the 'unconscious' organized structures that underlie not only the consciously organized discussions, but also those discussions of other matters that are influenced by or somehow implicated in the more specifically focused discourses. There are moments in *Othello* in which politics and religion are dealt with explicitly: in the Senate itself in Act 1, scene 3, for example, or in Iago's reference to Othello's having been baptized (2.3.338). Much more interesting from the point of view of psychoanalytical approaches to discourse are the moments in which the explicit discourses are not so evident, but their residual influence, as it were, can be discerned. We are looking for a shaping, or limiting power; a capacity to exert an influence over what seems to be common sense or just the way things are: 'nature' or 'reality' or 'the world'. We are looking for it in language and we are looking for what operates against it in the relationship we have as individual speakers with the language we speak, between what Benveniste calls 'enunciation' and the 'enounced'. If the 'enounced' belongs to language, it belongs so much the less to us as speakers, attempting to make sense of our experience, of ourselves and of the world as it seems to us, in the language which is our only language (however many languages we can speak) and which we did not make to suit ourselves. 'Enunciation', the act of speaking, has another 'I' as its subject: the 'I' that struggles to make itself understood to itself as well as to others: the 'enounced' implies an 'I' much more in keeping with the world as discourse would have it.

There is considerable disagreement about what the world is like in *Othello* and, most interestingly of all, Othello and Iago themselves vividly reveal what is at stake in such disagreements. When Iago, for example, is talking to Roderigo at the beginning of the play, he says, 'such a one do I profess myself' (1.1.54) and we realize that Iago is engaged in an act of subversive self-definition, culminating in the mysterious (and probably meaningless) 'I am not what I am' (1.1.64). He means to impress upon Roderigo that he is a subtle fellow, devious and slippery, but as the play goes on we see that defining himself matters very much to Iago: his soliloquies are almost explanations of himself, making clear his motives, the lights by which he guides himself. He is an independent thinker, an original, or at least he thinks he is, and presents himself to Roderigo as such. At 1.3.320ff. he presents a view of the moral life that daringly dismisses (at least it does so implicitly) the Christian framework and puts in its place a model of rational self-interest in pursuit of desires. At 1.1.40ff. he presents in his scathing account of servants who do their duty a social-political model of exploitation supported by ideology (the ideology of duty as a virtue) from which he claims to have freed himself and against which he pits himself and others like him as covertly practising against the master-class.

If we are not willing to resort to superstitious accounts of Iago as a devil (accounts which he himself encourages by his references to hell – 1.3.358 and 401 and again at 2.3.345 – not to mention the exchange between himself and Othello in Act 5, scene 2 at the end of the play), then we may want to seek to understand him as a subversive influence erupting out of the attempts of discourse to restrain, by making literally unspeakable, the disruptive forces to be found in the unconscious of the individual psyche and in the more consciously articulated aspirations of the oppressed in the social–political world. In such an account the demonization of Iago by the play may be seen to be the play's ingrained conservatism: fear of the subversive. From a progressive point of view such conservatism can be denounced. This is not to make a hero of Iago: it is to identify in the play a picture of what it is like to live within discourses we ourselves have outgrown and which we can therefore see more clearly than can any of those still enmeshed in their coils. Shakespeare's great originals, such as Macbeth, Iago and Edmund, do not come to good ends. It may be that Shakespeare himself privately toyed with some of the ideas he has them express, but that is a matter for historians and biographers. Criticism is trying to interpret texts, and that involves quite other goals.

Iago is not a real person: he is a character in a play. He exists as something constructed by readers as much as by actors from the guidance given by the script written for him, and by audiences from their response to the constructions offered for their enjoyment by actors, directors and theatre companies, working individually and collaboratively to put on plays. Our task as critics is to explore the text to the limits (as we know them; there may well be further limits of which we know nothing) to which interpretation will take us. When we have done this, we should try to make what consistent sense of what we have found out that we can. When we try to do that with Iago we may summarize by reflecting that in any social situation there is an unspoken and an unspeakable. The unspoken is what is by common consent left unsaid but which is thought. The unspeakable is what cannot be thought. That it cannot be thought does not mean that it does not exist; it may be thought in some form that denies its existence, literally or perhaps only effectively. Demonization has this consequence: that the thought is so fearful that it cannot be entertained but must be shunned.

Freud's account of repression is useful at such points as it gives us a means of imagining the psychological processes involved, the transformation of material into unconscious and conscious material, the residual presence of the unconscious and its baleful influence on the conscious. Iago is the unspeakable, the temptation to yield to the innocence of dreams and to live like that in the world. The consequence of this speaking the unspeakable is to expose the speakable in all its fragility so that we can see it as terribly (and wrongly) threatened by evil, or as a social construction, designed to keep certain people in their places, and wrongfully denying outlets to expression that, released from bondage, would expand our understanding of the human. What we do depends upon our own points of view, our personal beliefs, as critics. What may be true is that we cannot ignore the possibilities such readings propose.

Othello then becomes two plays: the play that is discussed by 'traditional' criticism, which is concerned with the doings of people as those are represented in dramatic form, the play's 'characters' as we call them; and a play in which what seem to be characters from one point of view become emblems of forces below and beyond 'characters', if by 'character' we mean something like an individual person. If by 'character' we mean what we mean when we speak of the 'characters' of an alphabet, or the 'characters' on a keyboard – that is, as a set of figures or designs that symbolize something – then we may continue to speak of the 'characters' of *Othello* while passing from one way of talking to another.

We must bear this in mind as we pass now to consider Desdemona: one of the most enigmatic of the 'characters', in either sense, of *Othello*.

CHAPTER 7

DESDEMONA: CHARACTER AND SIGN: 'THIS MOST GOODLY BOOK'

The critic G. Wilson Knight established a distinctive mode of analysis of Shakespeare's plays in a series of essays in the 1930s. His method was to treat the plays as poems as well as plays, and he did this by tracing patterns of imagery and bringing out the symbolic or even mythic significance of the plays. His treatment of *Othello* is particularly useful for the light it throws on Desdemona:

> *Othello* is eminently a domestic tragedy. But this element in the play is yet to be related to another more universal element. Othello is concretely human, so is Desdemona. Othello is very much the typical middle-aged bachelor entering matrimony late in life, but he is also, to transpose a phrase of Iago's, a symbol of human – especially masculine – 'purpose, courage, and valour' (4.2.216), and, in a final judgement, is seen to represent the idea of human faith and value in a very wide sense. Now Desdemona, also very human, with an individual domestic feminine charm and simplicity, is yet also a symbol of woman in general daring the unknown seas of marriage with the mystery of man. Beyond this, in the far flight of a transcendental interpretation, it is clear that she becomes a symbol of man's ideal, the supreme value of love. At the limit of the series of wider and wider suggestions which appear from imaginative contemplation of a poetic symbol she is to be equated with the divine principle. (Knight 1930, 108–9)

In the history of theatrical traditions a remarkable process is discernible: in the first place dramatic characters begin life as signs and become persons; in the second place persons become signs. Medieval theatre personified characteristics (such as Vice and Sin), thus creating characters: dramatic persons who embodied, and thus illustrated, the characteristics brought to dramatic life. The theatre of the Shakespeare's time, drawing on the theatre of Ancient Rome as well as on the native dramatic tradition, presented much more rounded characters.

This process may be linked with changing ideas of personhood. It has been argued (Belsey 1985) that in some works of Shakespeare's time there can be seen a distinctive kind of personality, an independent individual paying little heed to the customary morality and even to the laws of his or her time, preferring to pursue lights of his or her own making. If this is so then a consequence is that whereas the social world had until then been the stage towards which audiences looked to see the drama of the conflict between different ideas and characteristics being enacted, that stage is replaced by the minds of individual persons in which the conflicts are enacted. The mind becomes the stage. The distinction between individual person and social world begins to lose its force as the stimuli to, and the constraints upon, behaviour are exerted less by the world outside the individual person and more by forces within the individual person. Thus the conflicts that are at one time fought out within the discourses of the social world are at another fought out within the individual. So mythological kinds of thinking, and of presentation, are replaced by more realistic kinds of thinking and presentation.

However, a countervailing force is also observable: as we come to identify the world more and more with ourselves, so more and more do other persons come to exist for us only as signs or as blank tablets on which to write our own texts. When we come, as Iago has come to do, to write the rules for ourselves, to compose the scenarios for ourselves, and to assign meanings as we choose, then this is what happens: the others become actors in our dramas. William Hazlitt noticed this feature of Iago's behaviour in his *The Characters of Shakespeare's Plays*:

> He is an amateur of tragedy in real life; and instead of employing
> his invention on imaginary characters, or long-forgotten inci-

dents, he takes the bolder and more desperate course of getting up his plot at home, casts the principal parts among his nearest friends and connections, and rehearses it in downright earnest, with steady nerves and unabated resolution. (Hazlitt 1906, 42)

However, it is not only Iago who approaches people as potential characters in his play: Othello addresses Desdemona in a strikingly similar way: 'Was this fair paper, this most goodly book / Made to write "whore" upon?' (4.2.72–73). The image of a Desdemona as a 'book', a set of blank pages, for others to write their meanings on, fully expresses this notion of a person becoming a sign, and being treated as a mere signifier, the interpretation of the meaning of which is at the disposal of others. In the discipline of semiotics a sign is formally analysed into two component parts, neither of which can exist as such without the other: the 'signifier', or material component of a sign, and the 'signified', or meaning of the sign. An example used by Roland Barthes is effective: in certain courts in Ancient Greek societies, votes were cast by means of pebbles, coloured black or white. A black pebble, found on a beach or by a roadside, means nothing at all: placed in a jar at the culminating point of a trial in a court in Ancient Greece, it meant a vote for the death penalty. The meaning of the sign is not contained in the signifier but in the context in which it is placed. But without the signifier, the meaning could not take material shape. It follows that there is no necessary link between signifier and signified: that, had Ancient Greek courts so decided, a white pebble, or some other thing altogether, could have carried the meaning of a vote for the death penalty. It follows from this that meanings are maintained by convention and that where convention is not securely established the meaning ascribed to a signifier may change. A signifier may carry more than one meaning at any time; these meanings may be at cross-purposes. As Othello writes 'whore' upon the 'most goodly book' of Desdemona, others (including, and perhaps especially, ourselves as audiences and readers) write their own meanings upon her. We will ask whether there is any meaning attaching there by right. Is there a 'real' Desdemona?

When Jacques in *As You Like It* comments 'All the world's a stage, / And all the men and women merely players' (2.7.139–40), he is reminding the audience of a metaphor with which Shakespeare makes play quite frequently, perhaps nowhere quite so movingly as in Macbeth's bitter reflections upon hearing of the death of Lady Macbeth:

Life's [. . .] a poor player,
That struts and frets his hour upon the stage
And then is heard no more. (5.5.24–26)

Of course, the actors are real, real people; but Macbeth is not a real person, nor is Jacques, nor Desdemona: they are imaginary persons, invoked for us by real persons pretending to be the persons imagined by the person who wrote the words that person imagined that these imaginary persons would speak, at least as the persons pretending to be them imagine they are from those words. Clearly there is much room for interpretation, for 'getting it wrong'. As the plays, especially *Othello*, are so concerned with 'getting it wrong', there is the potential for a degree of self-referentiality. This means that the play offers images of itself, as though it were looking in a mirror; what happens on stage is mirrored by its happening on stage. There is a fine moment in *Twelfth Night* when, in the middle of the joke that is being played on Malvolio, Valentine says to the others playing the joke: 'If this were played upon a stage now, I could condemn it as an improbable fiction' (3.4.128–29). It is in fact being played upon a stage and it is in fact an improbable fiction. The effect is not the breaking of any spell though, because audiences are not, by and large, under any illusion that what they are watching is really happening. Samuel Johnson puts it very well: 'Imitations produce pain or pleasure not because they are mistaken for realities but because they bring realities to mind' (Johnson 1969, 71). Part of the pleasure of the stage is exactly that double vision that is available to us when we see both what is really happening and what is brought to mind by what is really happening. That effect is poignant in a tragedy: we see what is really happening, that an actor we may know from television is playing Desdemona, and we see at the same time what is being brought to mind – the grief, the happiness, of a person. That the person is imagined does not diminish for us one jot her being a person. We may reflect that all persons are imagined, in the sense that the only access we have to them is to picture them in our mind as a construction from what we have before us, their words, their actions, their appearance. It is a striking reflection that we know more of characters in novels, because we know all that there is to know about them, than we know of ourselves or of anybody else.

In this we are in the same position as the characters themselves: what we know is only what they can know – what people say and do. If they do not know what someone has said or done that is not because it is not something that they could have known but only something that they could have known but did not know. This is the basis of dramatic irony. Thus in a terrifying scene (4.2) Othello interrogates Desdemona, challenging her to admit her guilt, and she responds with sincere protestations of her innocence. We know that they are sincere: Othello is convinced that they are only further proofs of her duplicity, which is as audacious as it is extreme:

> OTHELLO: Are not you a strumpet?
> DESDEMONA: No, as I am a Christian.
> If to preserve this vessel for my lord
> From any hated foul unlawful touch
> Be not to be a strumpet, I am none.
> OTHELLO: What, not a whore?
> DESDEMONA: No, as I shall be saved.
> OTHELLO: Is't possible?
> DESDEMONA: O heaven, forgive us!
> OTHELLO: I cry you mercy then,
> I took you for that cunning whore of Venice
> That married with Othello. You! Mistress!
> > *Enter* Emilia
> That have the office opposite to Saint Peter
> And keeps the gates of hell – you, you, ay, you!
> We have done our course, there's money for your pains.
> I pray you, turn the key and keep our counsel.
> > *Exit* (4.2.83–96)

He has set up this fantastic play-acting at line 27:

> OTHELLO: [*to Emilia*] Some of your function, mistress,
> Leave procreants alone and shut the door;
> Cough, or cry hem, if anybody come.
> Your mystery, your mystery: nay, dispatch! (4.2.27–30)

He pretends that this is an assignation of lovers and Emilia the go-between bringing them together, and he ends the scene (or at least his part in it) by treating her as a sort of brothel-keeper, giving her money. He acts as though she were keeping their assignation a secret and keeping watch for them ('Cough, or cry hem, if anybody come') and then he pays her for her 'office opposite to Saint Peter', her watching at 'the gates of hell'.

It is a wonderful scene for Othello: it is his play that he has made up, and in which he stars as a mistreated man who is struggling to maintain his dignity and rise above the insult done to him. He achieves this by an elaborately staged apology for mistaken identity:

> I cry you mercy then,
> I took you for that cunning whore of Venice
> That married with Othello. (4.2.90–92)

I am sorry, he says, I thought you were my wife, Desdemona. When he walks off the stage he should have the applause of every member of the audience. Or rather he would have were he right about his situation, but he is not right: Desdemona is right, she is innocent, she is sincere. Othello has already prepared himself for such dissimulation however. He interrogates Emilia at the beginning of the scene:

> OTHELLO: You have seen nothing, then?
> EMILIA: Nor ever heard, nor ever did suspect.
> OTHELLO: Yes, you have seen Cassio and . . . she together.
> EMILIA: But then I saw no harm, and then I heard
> Each syllable that breath made up between them.
> OTHELLO: What, did they never whisper?

EMILIA: Never, my lord.
OTHELLO: Nor send you out o'th' way?
EMILIA: Never.
OTHELLO: To fetch her fan, her gloves, her mask, nor nothing?
EMILIA: Never, my lord.
OTHELLO: That's strange (4.2.1–11).

It is of course only strange if one is convinced that Desdemona is guilty of a sexual relationship with Cassio, but cannot see when and how it was being exercised. It is not at all strange if one drops the hypothesis of her guilt. Her Christian protestations do not help her either:

This is a subtle whore,
A closet, lock and key, of villainous secrets;
And yet she'll kneel and pray, I have seen her do't. (4.2.21–23)

Emilia 'says enough; yet she's a simple bawd / That cannot say as much' (4.2.20–21), so that proves nothing either. If we are convinced of something that cannot be proved because it is not so, we may find that it cannot be disproved either, because we can always extend our hypothesis to cover the awkward absence of proof positive.

Othello, having absorbed Iago's wisdom that 'in Venice they do let God see the pranks / They dare not show their husbands' (3.3.205–06), is now looking to find them out: not finding them out only convinces him of the cleverness with which they are being hid. This is terrifying. How could such a man be disabused?

If we step aside for a moment we can observe a parallel with two things: knowledge in general and a very specific form of knowledge. We may see *Othello* as a play about guilt and innocence and about suspicion and trust. We may see it also as a play about what we can know and what we must accept by faith. We can see it then as a play about the *hubris* implicit in certain kinds of knowledge-quest. What should we seek to know and what should we not seek to know? Second, and topically, we may see it as a parable about intelligence in the sense of espionage and the dangerous game of misinformation. Iago misleads Othello much as both sides sought to mislead each other during the Cold War. The parallels between the play and that situation may allow us to present it in the theatre, for example, in such a way as to make it appear to be 'about' the Cold War.

In much this way Othello makes his meeting with Desdemona appear to be an encounter in a brothel in hell. It isn't, we may argue, but he is convinced that it is. How can we be sure that things are not the way people think that they are? There are two aspects to this question: one dismisses the question fairly easily, and that is the aspect of evidence. We know that Desdemona is innocent. The other is much more difficult: in the absence of evidence we are in the realm of conviction:

> EMILIA: I durst, my lord, to wager she is honest,
> Lay down my soul at stake: if you think other
> Remove your thought, it doth abuse your bosom.
> If any wretch have put this in your head
> Let heaven requite it with the serpent's curse,
> For if she be not honest, chaste and true
> There's no man happy: the purest of their wives
> Is foul as slander. (4.2.12–19)

The question that lurks in the background all the time is, how do we know that Desdemona is innocent?

Put it the other way around. How do we know that anybody is innocent of some imputed crime? If we are unable to establish that it is not possible that whatever is alleged could have happened (because no opportunity can be hypothesized, for example), then we have to go on the absence of proof and the strength of our conviction. In fact we do not know that Desdemona is innocent: we *believe* that Desdemona is innocent. To be precise, if it is adultery of which she is accused, then there has been no opportunity; but if it is more generally alleged that she has had (and may want to continue, although she will not have been able to do anything about it during the play) sexual relations with Cassio, and even with others, then we do not know that she has not.

Her first appearance at 1.3.170 has her a silent presence on the stage during a short exchange between the Duke and Brabantio, significant because that exchange shows us that Desdemona's testimony is Brabantio's last hope. Her words are the end of that hope:

> My noble father,
> I do perceive here a divided duty.
> To you I am bound for life and education:
> My life and education both do learn me
> How to respect you; you are the lord of duty,
> I am hitherto your daughter. But here's my husband:
> And so much duty as my mother showed
> To you, preferring you before her father,
> So much I challenge that I may profess
> Due to the Moor my lord. (1.3.180–89)

She speaks a sentiment reminiscent of Cordelia's speech in *The Tragedy of King Lear*, and comparison is instructive:

> Good my lord,
> You have begot me, bred me, loved me. I
> Return those duties back as are right fit,
> Obey you, love you and most honour you.
> Why have my sisters husbands, if they say
> They love you all? Haply when I shall wed,
> That lord whose hand must take my plight shall carry
> Half my love with him, half my care and duty.
> Sure, I shall never marry like my sisters. (1.1.95–103)

So far the situations are distinct but comparable: Desdemona is married; Cordelia is speaking of marriage as a hypothetical prospect. This will explain her allowing her father the other half of her 'love' and of her 'care and duty'. Desdemona is married and her husband is 'preferred', not even granted an equal share in her love as Cordelia says. Most importantly, Cordelia's speech is a spirited, even mischievous, challenge to her sisters' rhetorical acts of devotion to their father, pointing out, rather rudely perhaps, the inherent and embarrassing contradiction contained in them (embarrassing because their husbands are present). The message is the same: fathers lose daughters to their sons-in-law. There is an old pattern here: the foolish *senex* (old man) of Roman comedy who tries in vain to hold on to youth, daughters and other girls, who are spirited away from his grasp by virile young men. It is the figure of Egeus from *A Midsummer Night's Dream* who is later, at the end of Shakespeare's career, redrawn entirely in Prospero in *The Tempest*, although not so completely redrawn that his lineaments cannot be made out at all.

Desdemona's speech is not a rejoinder to her father: it is a solicitous and sympathetic recognition of his feelings and of the inevitability of their being hurt, but it is also a quiet affirmation of the rightness, in her view, of her actions. It is more mature than Cordelia's, though it acknowledges the same parameters, uncannily closely:

> My noble father,
> I do perceive here a divided duty.
> To you I am bound for life and education:
> My life and education both do learn me
> How to respect you; you are the lord of duty,
> I am hitherto your daughter. (1.3.180–85)

And:

> Good my lord,
> You have begot me, bred me, loved me. I
> Return those duties back as are right fit,
> Obey you, love you and most honour you. (1.1.95–98)

It is the recognition of the fact of duty and of the nature of duty that unites these two, and the corollary recognition of the requirements of sexual love. Parental, and filial, love is one thing: sexual love is another. Duty may not be unpleasant, it may in fact be a pleasure. It will never rival the significance of sexual love and of marriage as the appropriate social vehicle of such love. This is not a personal preference: it is the expression of a law of nature, or at least of a social law so well established as to be as good as a natural law.

Brabantio immediately concedes defeat; gracelessly but prompt-ly: 'God be with you, I have done. / Please it your grace, on to the state affairs' (1.3.190–91). Desdemona stands by silently for a further 53 lines before she intervenes in the discussion of what should happen to her while Othello is off at Cyprus. She is being discussed as though she were so much baggage to be stowed somewhere, and she has to butt in to be heard. The Duke suggests she should stay at Brabantio's, but both Brabantio and Othello immediately object. So does Desdemona:

> Nor would I there reside
> To put my father in impatient thoughts
> By being in his eye. Most gracious duke,
> To my unfolding lend your prosperous ear
> And let me find a charter in your voice
> T'assist my simpleness. (1.3.242–47)

This is dignified and not at all assertive, and it is diplomatic. She calls the Duke 'gracious' and describes his ear as 'prosperous'; she offers of herself her 'simpleness'. This is graceful; it might also be clever.

She then says of herself some remarkable things:

> That I did love the Moor to live with him
> My downright violence and scorn of fortunes
> May trumpet to the world. My heart's subdued
> Even to the very quality of my lord:
> I saw Othello's visage in his mind,
> And to his honours and his valiant parts
> Did I my soul and fortunes consecrate,
> So that, dear lords, if I be left behind,
> A moth of peace, and he go to the war,
> The rites for which I love him are bereft me,
> And I a heavy interim shall support
> By his dear absence. Let me go with him. (1.3.249–60)

Her straightforwardness, her plainness, is what is remarkable in this speech. We should remember that all we have heard of

Desdemona is what her father has said of her and what Othello has said of her. Her father's views are as follows:

> A maid so tender, fair and happy,
> So opposite to marriage that she shunned
> The wealthy, curled darlings of our nation. (1.2.66–68)

And again:

> A maiden never bold,
> Of spirit so still and quiet that her motion
> Blushed at herself. (1.3.95–97)

Othello describes her indirectly. Having sketched the sorts of tales he told Brabantio, he says:

> This to hear
> Would Desdemona seriously incline,
> But still the house affairs would draw her thence,
> Which ever as she could with haste dispatch
> She'd come again, and with a greedy ear
> Devour up my discourse; which I, observing,
> Took once a pliant hour and found good means
> To draw from her a prayer of earnest heart
> That I would all my pilgrimage dilate,
> Whereof by parcels she had something heard
> But not intentively. I did consent,
> And often did beguile her of her tears
> When I did speak of some distressful stroke
> That my youth suffered. My story being done
> She gave me for my pains a world of sighs,
> She swore in faith 'twas strange, 'twas passing strange,
> 'Twas pitiful, 'twas wondrous pitiful;
> She wished she had not heard it, yet she wished
> That heaven had made her such a man. She thanked me
> And bade me, if I had a friend that loved her,
> I should but teach him how to tell my story
> And that would woo her. Upon this hint I spake:

> She loved me for the dangers I had passed
> And I loved her that she did pity them. (1.3.146–69)

The picture of Desdemona that this speech gives is of someone whose domestic duties cannot offer imaginative satisfaction; someone who is drawn by Othello's tales of a world outside the world she knows; someone who is prepared to take risks (Othello recounts how he 'often did beguile her of her tears / When I did speak of some distressful stroke / That my youth suffered'). The risks are the risks that imaginative people take. 'She wished she had not heard it' is particularly eloquent: the audience's own experience may well be summed up in this picture of imaginative excitement as, by the same token, the apparently contradictory 'yet she wished / That heaven had made her such a man' is equally understandable by anyone who has had an experience that has gripped and thrilled them.

This speech is a story about a story: Othello tells how he told a tale, and not just once, but several times. It is a story about the re-telling of a story. Its closure is enacted by the emergence of Desdemona onto the stage just as he has brought his narrative to an end. The conclusion of his story is the appearance of his wife. It is as though a master showman had contrived the moment:

> This only is the witchcraft I have used:
>> *Enter* Desdemona, Iago, *Attendants*
> Here comes the lady, let her witness it.
> DUKE: I think this tale would win my daughter, too. (1.3.170–72)

The story he tells to the Signiory (as he calls them) invites us to read between the lines: to see a girl chained by domesticity glimpsing space and freedom in these tales of a world outside Venice. We are not surprised that someone with such an imagination has rejected the 'wealthy, curled darlings of our nation' that an indulgent and hopeful father has paraded before her; we easily imagine her eagerness, the 'greedy ear' with which she 'devoured' Othello's tales.

The manoeuvring between them is almost comical: he 'Took once a pliant hour, and found good means / To draw from her a prayer of earnest heart / That I would all my pilgrimage dilate', and she 'bade me, if I had a friend that loved her, / I should but teach him how to tell my story / And that would woo her'. These clumsy mechanisms suggest novice lovers.

Othello's summary is poignant: 'She loved me for the dangers I had passed / And I loved her that she did pity them' (1.3.168–69). It must be compared with her own account:

> That I did love the Moor to live with him
> My downright violence and scorn of fortunes
> May trumpet to the world. My heart's subdued
> Even to the very quality of my lord:
> I saw Othello's visage in his mind,
> And to his honours and his valiant parts
> Did I my soul and fortunes consecrate. (1.3.249–55)

Othello is talking about how their love seems to him, and it is quite a contrast with Desdemona's account of her love for him. Iago's view is not irrelevant here: 'Mark me with what violence she first loved the Moor, but for bragging and telling her fantastical lies' (2.1.220–21). Desdemona does not mention Othello's storytelling: she says:

> I saw Othello's visage in his mind,
> And to his honours and his valiant parts
> Did I my soul and fortunes consecrate. (1.3.253–55)

This is not easy to make out. It seems to mean that Desdemona is in love with Othello himself, and not with his appearance or with any other part of him as a separable part of him. It is an affirmation of the wholeness and clear-sightedness of her love for him. Iago constantly asserts that it is a merely physical appetite, which will certainly tire; and he and Othello and Brabantio seem to agree that Othello's appearance ought to frighten rather than attract her (though Iago hints, to Othello as well as to Roderigo, that Desdemona's attraction to him is a mark of her perverse temperament).

Desdemona herself never ceases to affirm her love for him, for 'my lord' as she persistently calls him, even at the end: 'Commend me to my kind lord – O, farewell! (5.2.123). If Othello's love may be construed as Romantic, and perhaps immature, Desdemona's is less easy to characterize in this way. She is naïve: when she is discussing the lost handkerchief with Emilia she says:

> but my noble moor
> Is true of mind, and made of no such baseness
> As jealous creatures are, it were enough
> To put him to ill thinking.
> EMILIA: Is he not jealous?
> DESDEMONA: Who, he? I think the sun where he was born
> Drew all such humours from him. (3.4.26–31)

Then of course Othello enters and shortly starts to quiz her precisely about the lost handkerchief. This is dramatic irony. She is naïve again – and Shakespeare exploits again dramatic irony – when at the beginning of Act 3, scene 3 she insists on talking of Cassio to Othello, when to the audience it is obvious that something has disturbed him and he does not want to speak about Cassio at all. She is, finally, naïve when on the quayside at Cyprus she exchanges bawdy jests with Iago. Othello in Act 3, scene 4 addresses the subject of the palm of her hand:

> OTHELLO: Give me your hand. This hand is moist, my lady.
> DESDEMONA: It hath felt no age, nor known no sorrow.
> OTHELLO: This argues fruitfulness and liberal heart:
> Hot, hot and moist. This hand of yours requires
> A sequester from liberty, fasting, and prayer,
> Much castigation, exercise devout,
> For here's a young and sweating devil, here,
> That commonly rebels. 'Tis a good hand,
> A frank one. (3.4.36–44)

Whether these things are matters of unconscious, naïve, and innocent self-confidence, which a more watchful self-awareness would control or conceal, or really are signs of a lack of self-control, we never find out: Othello kills her before she can do, or not do, anything.

Desdemona's final scene with Emilia (4.3) is a marvellous, moving, complex moment. She has asked Emilia to put her wedding sheets on her bed (4.2.107), and Emilia at 4.3.20 tells Desdemona that she has done her bidding. Desdemona recalls a maid of her mother's, called Barbary, and a song she used to sing, having been deserted by a false lover. As Emilia dresses her for bed she talks to Desdemona about how handsome Lodovico is, and Desdemona sings to herself. It is an intimate, quiet, cosy moment. Desdemona cannot forget that Othello has called her a whore, and returns to the idea she has dismissed out of hand in the previous scene:

> I cannot say whore:
> It does abhor me now I speak the word;
> To do the act that might the addition earn
> Not the world's mass of vanity could make me. (4.2.163–66)

Now she questions Emilia whether 'there be women do abuse their husbands / In such gross kind? (4.3.61–62). She presses: 'Wouldst thou do such a deed for all the world?' (4.3.63), and Emilia, pressed, concedes that 'I would not do such a thing for a joint-ring [. . .] But for all the whole world? ud's pity, who would not make her husband a cuckold to make him a monarch? I should venture purgatory for't' (4.3.71–76). Such juggling is not for Desdemona: 'Beshrew me, if I would do such a wrong / For the whole world!' (4.3.77–78), and even after Emilia has made a spirited speech along the lines that men have only themselves to blame if they are let down, she concludes: 'Good night, good night. God me such usage send / Not to pick bad from bad, but by bad mend!' (4.3.103–04). She seems bewildered by Emilia's sophistication, and one can forgive the slightly moralizing tone with which she sets off to bed to await Othello.

We should consider the wedding sheets. Iago's urgent question from the first act hangs over the action now: 'are you fast married?' (1.2.11). Are the wedding sheets preparatory or celebratory? She asks Emilia to shroud her in one of these sheets should she die before Emilia dies (4.3.22–23). Her wedding bed is the scene of her murder: 'Strangle her in her bed – even the bed she hath contaminated' (4.1.204–05). Othello himself comments: 'Good, good, the justice of it pleases; very good!' (4.1.206). 'Justice' here is not a moral but an aesthetic matter, 'poetic justice'. Desdemona unwittingly colludes in the preparation of the scene of her ritual demise, her transformation from a young, sexually alert, vivid person to an idealized abstraction, a ghastly parody, a frozen corpse, a stone body.

It is very difficult to avoid the conclusion that she has got what the person Othello thinks she is deserves, at least in his eyes. It is also difficult to avoid the conclusion that he does not consistently think of her as this person but really struggles to idealize her another way, as he seems to be doing when he says: 'Look where she comes: / If she be false, O then heaven mocks itself' (3.3.281–82); or, again, later: 'she might lie by an emperor's side and command him tasks' (4.1.181–82); or a few lines after this last remark: 'O, she will sing the savageness out of a bear! of so high and plenteous wit and invention!' (4.1.185–87); or again: 'But yet the pity of it, Iago – O, Iago, the pity of it, Iago!' (4.1.192–93).

In the final scene Desdemona argues her case until she realizes that hope is lost when Othello tells her that Cassio is dead: 'Alas, he is betrayed, and I undone' (5.2.75). Does she realize that there is a plot against her? It would seem so. Her words, 'betrayed' of Cassio and 'undone' of herself, suggest that she sees that someone (does she realize that it is Iago? Her words are in response to Othello's 'his mouth is stopped. Honest Iago / Hath ta'en order for't' (5.2.71–72)) has plotted against them both, and suggest that she realizes also that Othello has been hoodwinked, because she never blames him.

She begs to be allowed to live, but even in her dying moments, when Emilia asks her 'O, who hath done / This deed?' (5.2.121–22) she replies, mysteriously: 'Nobody, I myself. Farewell. / Commend me to my kind lord – O, farewell!' (5.2.122–23). It is as if she thinks herself responsible, not for anything she has done, but for what she cannot help being. In Act 4, scene 3 she says to Emilia, 'O, these men, these men!' (4.3.59), as though she had had extensive experience. What can she mean? She says it just after she has said that her eyes itch and that she has heard that this means that she will weep, and just before she says:

> Dost thou in conscience think – tell me, Emilia –
> That there be women do abuse their husbands
> In such gross kind? (4.3.60–62)

It is possible to play this as curiosity and not appalled disbelief; as the first, tentative stirrings of inquisitiveness about the world on the part of a young, protected girl whose copybook morality may seem like a settled conviction, but may only be a frightened response to her first voyage out into a wider world than her father's parlour. Then the banter on the quayside shows us another possibility, that of a rather less strait-laced Desdemona. Her protestations that she could never imagine behaving as her husband believes that she has done become, in this other view, words uttered in a deliberate attempt to keep at bay a growing fascination, and her baffled rejection of Emilia's temporizing becomes less convincing as inability to accept what she is hearing than as unwillingness further to entertain talk of what she might begin to find decreasingly repugnant to her. When Emilia says, 'This Lodovico is a proper man. A very handsome man', Desdemona replies, 'He speaks well' (4.3.34–35). The scene is an echo of the exchange between Cassio and Iago in Act 2, scene 3:

> IAGO: He hath not yet made wanton the night with her, and she is sport for Jove.
> CASSIO: She's a most exquisite lady.
> IAGO: And I'll warrant her full of game.
> CASSIO: Indeed she's a most fresh and delicate creature.
> IAGO: What an eye she has! methinks it sounds a parley to provocation.
> CASSIO: An inviting eye; and yet methinks right modest.
> IAGO: And when she speaks is it not an alarum to love?
> CASSIO: She is indeed perfection.
> IAGO: Well, happiness to their sheets! (2.3.16–26)

Where Iago seeks always to put the conversation onto a level of vulgar sensuality, Cassio seeks to elevate it to a level of refined gallantry. Emilia describes Lodovico as 'proper'; and as 'handsome'.

Desdemona says 'he speaks well'. But what is she thinking? Does she know what she is thinking? Some editions, following the folio, give 4.3.34 to Desdemona, so it is she, not Emilia, who introduces the topic. This strengthens the view I am proposing here. To refer again to Charles Rycroft's thesis (1981), we may imagine that she is not keeping the boundary between the desires that we keep back in our unconscious life and those that we can permit entry into conscious life as carefully as she might. The polite world of Cassio's gallantry patrols this boundary very carefully, and Iago prowls around the margins of the camp ready to seize the unwary, as that scene goes on to show. Freud and others found out that the process of discipline and self-control had gone much further in our own time and had set up the camp and its boundaries and its prowling wild animals in our own minds.

Jan Kott says that: 'Desdemona is sexually obsessed with Othello, but all men – Iago, Cassio, Roderigo – are obsessed with Desdemona. They remain in her erotic climate' (1967, 94–5). Iago in Act 2 mutters aside as Cassio and Desdemona talk privately apart:

> He takes her by the palm; ay, well said, whisper. With as little a web as this will I ensnare as great a fly as Cassio. Ay, smile upon her, do: I will gyve thee in thine own courtesies. You say true, 'tis so indeed. If such tricks as these strip you out of your lieutenantry, it had been better you had not kissed your three fingers so oft, which now again you are most apt to play the sir in. Very good, well kissed, and excellent courtesy: 'tis so indeed! Yet again, your fingers to your lips? would they were clyster-pipes for your sake! (2.1.167–77)

Of course Iago is continuing the narrative of his plotting but he is also, and perhaps a little uncharacteristically, revealing, instead of expressing, his rage. The troubled rhythms of his speech are a little like what Othello's will become under his baleful influence later on, and his closing remark bears explanation. 'Clyster-pipes', the *OED* tells us, were tubes by means of which medicines were introduced into the rectum. Iago is identifying what, in his view, underlies all social graces: the innocence of dreams; the fancies that haunt the margins of the waking world. We may say that this is Iago's imagination only: but the psychoanalytical tradition will remind us that it is not only Iago who imagines the world in this way – we all do, only we do not know that we do except when in the heavily-coded language of dreams we may glimpse some of that buried life. Perhaps Iago is only someone in whom the awareness has not been so repressed that he can genuinely say that it never crossed his mind.

Desdemona of course cannot be held responsible for being the object of desire. Her erotic climate is not her fault. Even were she to exploit it consciously, those who overstepped the mark would be to blame – not what they would blame for their behaviour. Othello's speech (5.2./–22) expresses all the hopeless attempts to divert blame onto the object of desire that characterize the shameful equivocation with desire of all the men who come within that climate, and it is not edifying to watch. Her fatal resignation perhaps contains an element of knowledge of the effect she has had, possibly entirely unwittingly; if not entirely unwittingly, then perhaps not deliberately; if deliberately, then perhaps without, almost certainly, anything like a full knowledge of possible consequences. It is at worst a delightful consciousness of influence, a return, perhaps for the influence exerted by Othello over her. Desdemona cannot help being made into a sign, and she cannot determine her signification. Tragedy necessarily raises questions of agency: to what extent can we control ourselves and what other people make of us? It remains for us to consider some of the minor characters.

CHAPTER 8

THE IMPORTANCE OF THE MINOR CHARACTERS

Some of Shakespeare's finest touches are displayed in his minor characters. There are in *Othello* some minor characters we easily, and rightly, forget: the Clown is one; there are also some minor characters, and Emilia is chief among these, who rank among Shakespeare's finest creations in this field. Each has a part to play and that part is sometimes of great significance. From this point of view, we may start with the Duke, to illustrate a method of approach.

The Duke only appears in one scene and says very little, but his appearance is important. The play is subtitled 'The Moor of Venice'; the opening Act is set in Venice; it is the war between the Ottoman Turks and Venice that sends Othello and Desdemona to Cyprus; Othello's loyalty is to Venice and his great pride is that he served there: Venice is at the centre of the play. The Duke is at the centre of Venice.

Branbantio counters Roderigo and Iago as they shout at his window with a most memorable conviction: 'What tell'st thou me of robbing? This is Venice: / My house is not a grange' (1.1.104–05). 'This is Venice' speaks volumes. 'My house is not a grange': I do not live in the country where I may expect to be threatened; I live in the town where I expect to be protected. Venice, presided over by the Duke, protected by its armies, commanded by Othello, is safe. However, as he is about to find out, such safety depends on the reliability of the guardians of safety, Othello chief among them, and also on the probity of its political governors, and the Duke is chief among these.

Act 1, scene 3 starts with a sense of agitation: news is coming in but it is contradictory. The Duke is concerned. The entry of Brabantio and Othello is greeted with relief, but the Duke quickly learns that Brabantio has not come to contribute to the talk of war: he has other matters on his mind. To his great credit the Duke immediately devotes his entire attention to the reverend senator, promising faithfully that:

> Whoe'er he be, that in this foul proceeding
> Hath thus beguiled your daughter of herself,
> And you of her, the bloody book of law
> You shall yourself read, in the bitter letter,
> After your own sense, yea, though our proper son
> Stood in your action. (1.3.66–71)

Brabantio announces that Othello is the guilty party and the whole scene changes, as we have seen in Chapter 1. The Duke is faced with a problem: he needs Othello to manage the war but he cannot go back on his word to Brabantio. He invites Othello to defend himself and when Othello is introducing Desdemona, before she has a chance to speak, the Duke intervenes:

> I think this tale would win my daughter too.
> Good Brabantio, take up this mangled matter at the best:
> Men do their broken weapons rather use
> Than their bare hands. (1.3.172–75)

Brabantio begs the Duke to let Desdemona speak; he is disappointed by her speech; he gives in. The Duke then offers to heal the breach:

> Let me speak like yourself, and lay a sentence
> Which as a grise or step may help these lovers
> Into your favour.
> When remedies are past the griefs are ended
> By seeing the worst which late on hopes depended.
> To mourn a mischief that is past and gone
> Is the next way to draw new mischief on.

What cannot be preserved when fortune takes,
Patience her injury a mockery makes.
The robbed that smiles steals something from the thief,
He robs himself who spends a bootless grief. (1.3.200–10)

These phrases strike the listener as *cliché* (from the French, meaning 'stereotype', that word meaning, in turn, solid type blocks, for printing, and hence replicated images produced by type processes); they are not new thoughts, original thoughts, arresting thoughts: they are the sort of proverbial wisdom one might expect to find on greetings cards expressing condolence (and which one would not choose to receive). It is an extraordinary moment in a scene packed tight with extraordinary moments. It is a moment of skill and tact on Shakespeare's part, as the interpretative possibilities are rich. The drama of the speech is not its content but its form. The Duke must settle the matter. Brabantio cannot win and must be pacified in his loss. The Duke's message is not so much the condolence conveyed by his sentiments as it is the formal implication that this is ordinary: daily, mundane, typical. It is not worth new words. Brabantio replies bitterly (as we shall see in a moment) and the Duke turns straight away to prose and to talk of the war. The contrast between the rhyming couplets of such dull insensitive ordinariness and the sinewy prose of *realpolitik* is dramatically exhilarating. What he says is revealing:

The Turk with a most mighty preparation makes for Cyprus. Othello, the fortitude of the place is best known to you, and, though we have there a substitute of most allowed sufficiency, yet opinion, a sovereign mistress of effects, throws a more safer voice on you. You must therefore be content to slubber the gloss of your new fortunes with this more stubborn and boisterous expedition. (1.3.222–29)

The Duke does not say that he personally has chosen Othello, and he says, indeed, that 'we have there a substitute of most allowed sufficiency', but rather that 'opinion [. . .] throws a more safer voice on you'. This is not just a delicate regard for Montano's feelings: it is the Duke's frank acknowledgement that his job is to weigh options and to be guided by a collective wisdom. Venice was an oligarchy, not a monarchy: the Duke was a *primus inter pares* ('first among equals') and not an absolute ruler. He is expressing a considered and reflective summing-up of the situation.

This is a world away from the romantic independence we glimpse in Othello's account of himself that he just gave before the assembled senators. It is real politics: give and take, compromise, collective wisdom. It is unglamorous. The Duke has power, but it is embedded power, compromised by the world in which it operates. He cannot just decide for Othello because it suits him to: he has to find a way of winning support and achieving a compromise. Othello, all through the play, is individually, independently powerful. That is his undoing as it happens, but it is his great strength as well. The Duke acts as a foil to Othello in this crucial scene: standing for, embodying, the object of Othello's loyal service, he is, ironically, revealed as less powerful than his servant, less free to manoeuvre, less in command.

Brabantio sarcastically parodies the Duke in a moment striking in its dramatic focus:

> So let the Turk of Cyprus us beguile,
> We lose it not so long as we can smile;
> He bears the sentence well that nothing bears
> But the free comfort which from thence he hears.
> But he bears both the sentence and the sorrow
> That, to pay grief, must of poor patience borrow.
> These sentences to sugar or to gall,
> Being strong on both sides, are equivocal.
> But words are words: I never yet did hear
> That the bruised heart was pierced through the ear.
> I humbly beseech you, proceed to th'affairs of state.
> (1.3.211–21)

We may surmise that Brabantio understands too well what is at stake in this exchange: 'So let the Turk of Cyprus us beguile, / We lose it not so long as we can smile' (1.3.211–12). This is tantamount to saying, 'so I can lose my daughter as long as Venice doesn't lose

Cyprus?' And, of course, he is right. The play reminds us, as does *Macbeth* (1606?), how uncomfortable is the relationship between the state and those upon whom it relies to protect it from its enemies. Brabantio's reversion to prose in his closing line, 'I humbly beseech you, proceed to th'affairs of state' (1.3.221), not only signals his acceptance of the state of things but also effects a seamless transition into the Duke's prose instructions to Othello. The moment has passed. It is brought strikingly into focus and then it passes. 'State affairs' have brushed aside personal pain and indignity.

Just before the Duke has formally brought this encounter to a close with his 'sentence', there is a wonderfully crafted moment in which Brabantio expresses, with notable decorum, all the pain and indignity he feels. After Desdemona has made her feelings clear, Brabantio replies:

> God be with you, I have done.
> Please it your grace, on to the state affairs;
> I had rather to adopt a child than get it.
> Come hither, Moor:
> I here do give thee that with all my heart
> Which, but thou hast already, with all my heart
> I would keep from thee. For your sake, jewel,
> I am glad at soul I have no other child,
> For thy escape would teach me tyranny
> To hang clogs on them. I have done, my lord. (1.3.190–99)

This is a fine speech: a generous speech, full of good, telling detail. I especially like the way that the loving name 'jewel' is given as the tail-end of the line in which it is spoken; a line that is, in addition, metrically irregular. It appears almost as an afterthought, or as some final moment such as a farewell; a last thing said as someone is leaving. This is a fine example of Shakespeare's art as a dramatist using verse. Brabantio is no longer the foolish *senex* of Roman comedy (compare Egeus in *A Midsummer Night's Dream*) but a dignified and wounded man who generously gives up what he has lost. The Duke's incursion is redundant: Brabantio's repeated 'I have done' is a clear dramatic indicator that he has accepted the inevitable with good grace, but also with sadness. He has already said, we note, 'Please it your grace, on to the state affairs' (1.3.191), and he has to repeat it at line 221 before he is heeded. In this light the Duke's speech may be seen as a determined attempt – and, it must be said, a successful one – to regain control of the moment in the interests of 'the state affairs'; Brabantio's sarcasm is a reminder of the claims of the personal life against those of the public arena.

Emilia is at the opposite end of the scale from these two. Samuel Johnson described her most astutely and concisely as follows: 'The virtue of *Emilia* is such as we often find, worn loosely but not cast off, easy to commit small crimes but quickened and alarmed at atrocious villainies' (Johnson 1969, 143). She is remembered as the cause of all Desdemona's woes, for she it is who finds the handkerchief and conveys it to Iago, and she does it for no reason that she understands:

> What he will do with it
> Heaven knows, not I,
> I nothing, but to please his fantasy. (3.3.301–03)

She knows that this is wrong:

> If it be not for some purpose of import
> Give't me again. Poor lady, she'll run mad
> When she shall lack it. (3.3.320–22)

She is more loyal to her husband than she is to her mistress, though she feels sympathetically towards her. She lies when Desdemona discovers the loss:

> DESDEMONA: Where should I lose that handkerchief, Emilia?
> EMILIA: I know not, madam. (3.4.23–24)

She starts here to come forward a little in the play. So far she has been helpful to the plot in unnoticed ways: now she starts to emerge as a person with views. She queries Desdemona's confidence that Othello is not jealous:

EMILIA: Is not this man jealous?
DESDEMONA: I ne'er saw this before,
Sure there's some wonder in this handkerchief;
I am most unhappy in the loss of it.
EMILIA: 'Tis not a year or two shows us a man.
They are all but stomachs, and we all but food:
They eat us hungerly, and when they are full
They belch us. (3.4.100–07)

This is a belated answer to some of Iago's similarly stereotypical remarks from Act 2, scene 1 on the quayside at Cyprus, and it reminds us of that backdrop of conventional wisdom concerning relationships between men and women against which the love of Othello and Desdemona is pitched by the play, at least at first. The cynical reductionism of Iago ('It is merely a lust of the blood and a permission of the will' (1.3.335–36)) is an extreme version of this conventional wisdom. We are invited to hope that Othello and Desdemona will prove these cynics wrong.

Emilia serves in this scene to remind the audience of the significance of jealousy:

But jealous souls will not be answered so:
They are not ever jealous for the cause,
But jealous for they're jealous. It is a monster
Begot upon itself, born on itself. (3.4.159–62)

This seems surprisingly accurate, though critics and audiences have quarrelled over whether or not Othello is jealous since the earliest days. Coleridge (1969) and A. C. Bradley (1991) insist that he was not: F. R. Leavis (1937) insists that he is. As audiences we know that Othello's fears are built only on Iago's suspicions and, though we further know that Iago has made up his suspicions, we must never forget that Iago only voices what are his suspicions and he never actually attempts to pass off on Othello any evidence of a direct nature. The nearest he gets is his tale of Cassio's dream which, though undoubtedly a lie, is only a lie about hearing Cassio dream about Desdemona and which demonstrates nothing, as he points out himself: it is Othello who insists that it is evidence.

Emilia is quizzed by Othello at the beginning of Act 4, scene 2 and accused of having 'the office opposite to Saint Peter' (4.2.93), and it is in the immediate aftermath of this terrible exchange between Othello and Desdemona that she unwittingly hits on the truth:

> EMILIA: I will be hanged if some eternal villain
> Some busy and insinuating rogue,
> Some cogging, cozening slave, to get some office,
> Have not devised this slander, I will be hanged else!
> IAGO: Fie, there is no such man, it is impossible.
> DESDEMONA: If any such there be, heaven pardon him.
> EMILIA: A halter pardon him, and hell gnaw his bones!
> Why should he call her whore? who keeps her company?
> What place, what time, what form, what likelihood?
> The Moor's abused by some most villainous knave,
> Some base notorious knave, some scurvy fellow.
> O heaven, that such companions thou'dst unfold
> And put in every honest hand a whip
> To lash the rascals naked through the world
> Even from the east to th' west.
> IAGO: Speak within doors.
> EMILIA: O, fie upon them! some such squire he was
> That turned your wit the seamy side without
> And made you to suspect me with the Moor.
> IAGO: You are a fool, go to. (4.2.132–50)

This is a wonderfully tense moment: Emilia has summed up exactly what has happened and is choosing, without knowing it, the very language to irritate as well as to alarm her husband, as it is the language of common contempt and, as Coleridge brilliantly surmised (and was discussed in Chapter 4), it is the dread of contempt that motivates men who enjoy contempt for others, as Iago so clearly does for Roderigo, for example. Emilia emerges from this set of speeches as a much more clear-cut figure, roused by righteous indignation against what has been done to her mistress, fuelled by the memory that it has been done to her. A new light is thrown on Iago too as we see that what he has treated so lightly ('I know not if't be true, / But I for mere suspicion in that kind / Will do as if for surety' (1.3.387–89)) has probably really rankled.

Emilia is forthright at the end of the 'Willow Song' scene (4.3) in her defence of women's taking their revenges upon men who have treated them poorly, but it is upon her discovery of her dying mistress and the revelation that follows horrifyingly quickly that she is at her finest. She challenges Othello bravely, showing no fear, only righteous defiance in the face of such an 'atrocious villainy', to use Johnson's phrase, and she does it again, fatally for her, when her husband's plot is revealed. If we are looking for moral centres in *Othello* it is in such moments as Emilia's resistance to 'atrocious villainy' that we find it.

We find it also in Montano and Lodovico: decent people whose presence, though almost unnoticed, reminds us of the standards of judgement by which Venice lives, which is what drew Othello to it in the first place, we may assume. The complexity of the picture we are offered by the play would be much reduced if it were not for such moments as Lodovico's arrival at Cyprus, and Othello's striking Desdemona in front of him, and that bitter-sweet moment's conversation between Emilia and Desdemona in Act 4, scene 3 that has Lodovico as its subject: a delicate flirting with just the faintest hint of a possibility that reminds us how much Desdemona has already sacrificed in her determination to marry the man she has committed herself to, and what a terrible waste of a young life will be the result of these closing scenes in which the audience now knows it irretrievably finds itself.

In the end it is this matter of the closing moments with which any critical account must concern itself. Whatever Critical Theoretical perspective one adopts it is with the culminating impact of the work that one must engage. Marxists must show how their analysis in terms of class struggle can cope with it; psychoanalytical critics and feminists must show what light they can throw on its meaning; New Historicists and others must show that their insights will be able to take into account the completion of the work, towards which it has been moving, which has been taking shape from the very opening phrases.

The perspective that has not so far been much explored is the view from the postcolonial position. This body of theory looks at the way British culture describes its own colonialist activities as well as looking at the way British culture impacted upon the cultures of colonized peoples. It is perhaps this perspective that offers the most poignant view of the play. If there is much truth in Othello's last words then it will have to do with the glimpse they give of the origins of his relationship with Venice. We need to spell out for ourselves what he was doing in Aleppo 'once'; how old he was; what it has to do with his baptism (attested to by Iago, of all witnesses in such a matter surely the most reliable, at 2.3.338); his having lived a soldier's life 'since these arms of mine had seven years' pith' (1.3.84); and, most mysteriously, of his claim to 'fetch [his] life and being / From men of royal siege' (1.2.21–22). The last of course may only mean that his race is a noble race and not specifically that he is himself the descendant of kings; but we are still faced with the mystery of his origins and career to which he returns at his end.

One version we may tell is of the young, idealistic member of a subaltern race, colonial subject of a wealthy and militarily impressive overseas power, who dreams of serving the very power that has oppressed and exploited his people. Such a tale belongs in the imperialist narratives of nineteenth-century English popular fiction, for example, but may make sense of *Othello* and add a particular sadness to his end, as he has been so bewildered and misled by the power he idealized. A similar sadness attaches to Marxist accounts that emphasize the ideological attachments that bind people against their true interests in the service of the master class.

There is less flexibility in New Historicism to accommodate a tragic perspective, concerned as it is to discover the nature of the past and to uncover the partisan and judgmental nature of some critical attitudes towards the past; and psychoanalytical accounts tend towards a similar objectivity, which denies them any real eloquence when it comes to tragedy (though Freud's work itself uncovers an increasingly tragic vision of the human predicament). Feminism is particularly well suited to draw out the tragedies of both Desdemona and Emilia, trapped within a patriarchal ideology that allows them only to choose varieties of imprisonment or condemnation as whores; but it is perhaps as well able to elaborate Othello's tragedy as one of a constructed masculinity, which determines that he will have to decide between his love and his anxiety, condemning him to react to his anxiety by hating what he loves and driving him to make up a story about justice and vengeance. Such an analysis may even be able to extend itself to embrace Iago.

This study will not risk committing itself to any one of these points of view, but will briefly consider a scene that will surely have to be discussed in any attempt to give a final account of this uneasy work.

THROUGH THE CHARACTERS TO THE KEY THEMES AND ISSUES

Tragedies are all about endings. In each of Shakespeare's great tragedies, *Hamlet*, *Othello*, *King Lear* and *Macbeth*, the audience is invited to make a judgement of the central character, though that judgement is never straightforward. In the case of *Othello* the process is signalled by Lodovico's words:

> O thou Othello, that wert once so good,
> Fallen in the practice of a cursed slave,
> What shall be said to thee? (5.2.288–90)

Othello replies:

> Why, anything;
> An honourable murderer, if you will,
> For nought I did in hate, but all in honour. (5.2.290–92)

Earlier, Lodovico has called him 'this rash and most unfortunate man' (5.2.280) and the word 'unfortunate' echoes through the last part of this last scene. It all seems to have gone so terribly wrong. This, perhaps, is the essence of tragedy as Aristotle described it: misfortune. What then, as Lodovico asks, shall be said?

Cassio has the last word. This is appropriate: it was he who was the cause, in great part, of Iago's anger; it was he who, next to Desdemona and before Roderigo, was most wronged. He is heart-breakingly generous. Lodovico confronts Othello: 'This wretch hath part confessed his villainy. / Did you and he consent in Cassio's death?' (5.2.293–94). Othello responds with a muted 'Ay' and Cassio says: 'Dear general, I never gave you cause' (5.2.296). This is the simple truth. There never was anything in it. Desdemona has been traduced and murdered, and Cassio has been demoted, suspected, plotted against and wounded, all for nothing. Yet the penultimate words of the play are Cassio's. As Othello dies Cassio says: 'This did I fear, but thought he had no weapon, / For he was great of heart' (5.2.358—59). If we can only plumb the depths of the meaning of 'For he was great of heart' then we shall have resolved at last all the difficulties, contradictions and seeming asymmetries of the play, for the 'cause' (to use the word as Othello uses it at 5.2.1) is just this: 'he was great of heart'. But plumbing the depths of meaning is something that cannot actually be undertaken except as a project: it will never be completed. Everyone who encounters the play has to undertake the task, and no one will come away with a final answer. The contradiction at the heart of the play is in this notion of 'heart' itself, and in particular in the 'greatness' of it that Othello possesses, for in it may be discovered generosity and love but also anger and passionate jealousy and hatred. Only someone who does not feel at all will escape this contradiction.

This discussion of this moment in the play focuses all the concerns of this book, for, if audiences and readers are moved by Cassio's words, they may reflect that they are, after all, only words, and, in addition, that they are words about words, not about people, for none of these people exists. Critical appreciation acknowledges the skill of the author and of the actors and of the director: Critical Theory interrogates the text; audiences and readers are engaged, their feelings are aroused, their reflection stimulated. All of this occurs because of the arrangement of words that is the script for the play. This book has guided the reader through a range of ways of approaching those words and the point of it all has been to insist that your response as a reader of the play should be as thoughtful, reflective and open to interrogation as are the words to which you are responding.

The foregoing chapters have shown the reader how the characters take shape and to what ends, and have impressed upon the reader the openness of interpretation that such a view allows, and perhaps even demands. Finally, the reader should remember that texts are composed of interrelated and interacting strands of signifying possibilities and that as readers, performers or audience members we are always involved in a process of creating, from the hints we take from the text or from the performance, what we come to see as the characters and their meanings. In the end, the emotional impact of a work resides to a very important extent in our own creation of that work – or, rather, re-creation of that work – in our own minds.

FURTHER READING

The following list is a short selection of texts to start your reading. There are many student guides to *Othello*: a few are selected below. It is always better to read more than one so that you can compare views and develop your own arguments.

Bloom, Harold, ed. (1996), *William Shakespeare's 'Othello'*. New York: Chelsea House Publishers.

Bromham, Tony (1988), *'Othello' by William Shakespeare*. Hampshire: Palgrave Macmillan.

Mason, Pamela (2002), *Cambridge Student Guide to 'Othello'*. Cambridge: Cambridge University Press.

Salgado, Gamini and Fenella Salgado (1989), *Shakespeare's 'Othello'*. Harmondsworth: Penguin Books.

Simpson, Matt (2003), *Student Guide to Shakespeare's 'Othello'*. Greenwich Exchange.

The following two are guides to the play in performance and are useful correctives to the more literary critical approach usual in student guides:

Hankey, Julie (2005), *Othello*. Cambridge: Cambridge University Press.

Potter, Lois (2002), *Othello*. Manchester: Manchester University Press.

Lastly there are collections of critical essays. Selected below are two titles in the *Casebook* series: the *New Casebook* edited by

Lena Cowen Orlin complements John Wain's collection of earlier material. Nicholas Potter's *Reader's Guide to Essential Criticism* provides generous selections from key critical essays, with a linking commentary.

Orlin, Lena Cowen, ed. (2003), *Othello*. Hampshire: Palgrave Macmillan.

Potter, Nicholas, ed. (2000), *Shakespeare: 'Othello': A Reader's Guide to Essential Criticism*. Hampshire: Palgrave Macmillan.

Wain, John, ed. (1994), *Shakespeare: 'Othello'*. Hampshire: Palgrave Macmillan.

BIBLIOGRAPHY

PRIMARY

Freud, Sigmund (1954), *The Interpretation of Dreams*, translated by James Strachey. London: George Allen and Unwin.

Freud, Sigmund (1962), *Three Essays on the Theory of Sexuality*, translated by James Strachey. New York: Basic Books.

Shakespeare, William (1975), *As You Like It*, ed. Agnes Latham. London: Arden Shakespeare.

Shakespeare, William (1979), *A Midsummer Night's Dream*, ed. Harold F. Brooks. London: Arden Shakespeare.

Shakespeare, William (1997), *King Lear*, ed. R. A. Foakes. London: Arden Shakespeare.

Shakespeare, William (1951), *Macbeth*, ed. Kenneth Muir. London: Arden Shakespeare.

Shakespeare, William (1997), *Othello*, ed. E. A. J. Honigmann. London: Arden Shakespeare.

Shakespeare, William (1975), *Twelfth Night*, ed. J. M. Lothian and T. W. Craik. London: Arden Shakespeare.

SECONDARY

Belsey, Catherine (1985), *The Subject of Tragedy: Identity and Difference in Renaissance Drama*. London and New York: Methuen.

Bradley, A. C. (1991), *Shakespearean Tragedy*. Harmondsworth: Penguin.

Coleridge, Samuel Taylor (1969), ed. T. Hawkes, *Coleridge on Shakespeare*. Harmondsworth: Penguin.

Dollimore, Jonathan, and Alan Sinfield, eds (1985), *Political Shakespeare*. Manchester: Manchester University Press.

Empson, William (1951), *The Structure of Complex Words*. London: Chatto and Windus.

Felman, S. (1981), 'Re-reading feminity', *Yale French Studies* 62: 19–44.

Gardner, Helen (1968), '*Othello*: a retrospect, 1900–1950', *Shakespeare Survey* 24.

Hazlitt, William (1906), *The Characters of Shakespeare's Plays*. London: Dent.

Hobbes, Thomas (1998), *Leviathan*. Oxford: Oxford University Press.

Holderness, Graham (1985), *Shakespeare's History*. Hampshire: Palgrave Macmillan.

Johnson, Samuel (1969), ed. W.K. Wimsatt, *Johnson on Shakespeare*. Harmondsworth: Penguin.

Kott, Jan (1967), *Shakespeare Our Contemporary* (2nd edn). London: Routledge.

Knight, G. Wilson (1930), *The Wheel of Fire*. London: Oxford University Press.

Leavis, F. R. (1972), *Nor Shall My Sword*. London: Chatto and Windus.

Leavis, F. R. (1937), 'Diabolic intellect and the noble hero: a note on *Othello*', *Scrutiny* 6:3 (December 1937), 259–83.

Orkin, Martin (1987), 'Othello and the "plain face" of racism', *Shakespeare Quarterly* 38:2, 166–88.

Rycroft, Charles (1981), *The Innocence of Dreams*. Oxford: Oxford University Press.

Rymer, Thomas (1956), 'A Short View of Tragedy', in *The Critical Works of Thomas Rymer*, ed. Curt A. Zimansky. New Haven: Yale University Press.

Traub, Valerie (1992), *Desire and Anxiety: Circulations of Sexuality in Shakespearean Drama*. London and New York: Routledge.

Wimsatt, William K. and Monroe C. Beardsley (1946), 'The intentional fallacy', *Sewanee Review* 54, 468–88 (revised and republished in Wimsatt and Beardsley, 1954).

Wimsatt, William K. and Monroe C. Beardsley (1954), *The Verbal Icon: Studies in the Meaning of Poetry*. Lexington, Kentucky: University of Kentucky Press.

INDEX

actor(s) 2–3, 8–9, 15, 19,
    23, 31–2, 40, 83,
    86–7, 90, 92, 122
  acting 40, 61
    play-acting 94
    acting company 2
advertising 31
alterity 43
antiquity 12
aristocracy 12, 64, 67
Aristotle 36, 64, 121
audience 9, 12, 18, 22, 26,
    28–9, 31, 34, 37, 50,
    54, 59, 63, 71, 78,
    82–4, 87, 90–2, 94,
    101, 103, 115, 117,
    121–3

Barthes, Roland 91
bawdy 17, 103
Beardsley, Monroe C
    65
Belsey, Catherine 90
Benveniste, Émile 70, 83,
    85
bourgeois 67

Brabantio 1, 6–8, 11, 13,
    15–18, 20, 22, 43, 45,
    68–9, 84, 96–7, 99, 100,
    102, **109–14**
Bradley, A. C. 12, 28, 31, 36,
    40–1, 43, 46, 56, 62, 67,
    115

capitalism 12, 67
Cassio 2, 5, 14, 25, 27, 29, 30,
    32, 37, 39, 55, 57–8,
    78–9, 82, 94–6, 103,
    105–7, 115, 121–2
chivalry 12
Cinthio 1
cliché 16, 111
Coleridge, Samuel Taylor
    28, 31, 36, 40–1,
    43, 46, 49, 50–3,
    56, 62, 67,
    115–16
Cold War 96
coup de théâtre 40
creativity 21
Critical Theory 64–6, 69, 77,
    117, 122

psychoanalytical criticism
117

quarto 1622 1, 2

rational 47, 54, 86
reason 47, 53–4, 64, 69, 79, 81
reductionism 54, 59, 115
rhetoric 43, 54, 58, 97
rhyming couplets 16, 53, 111
Roderigo 1, 6–7, 10–11, 14,
17, 39, 45, 50–5, 58–9,
68–9, 78–9, 84–6, 102,
107, 109, 116, 121
Rycroft, Charles 79, 107
Rymer, Thomas 37, 63–4,
78–9, 83

science 54
semiotics 91
service 11–12, 59, 112, 118
sexuality 11, 43, 45–6, 72, 84
sexual desire 7, 11, 43, 45–6,
68–9, 71–3, 80, 82, 84,
98, 107
Shakespeare 1–2, 9, 12–14,
19–22, 28, 30–2, 41,
44–5, 49–51, 62–4, 70,
77, 86, 89–90, 92, 98,
103, 109, 111, 113, 121
*A Midsummer Night's
Dream* 16, 98, 113
As You Like It 22, 91–2
Hamlet 1, 50, 121
King Lear 1, 59, 80, 86,
97–8, 121
Macbeth 1, 22, 86, 92, 113,
121

Richard III 62
The Tempest 98
Titus Andronicus 1
Twelfth Night 92
sign 3, 42, 61, 89–91, 108, 123
signifieds 42, 91
signifiers 42, 91
Signiory 8, 10–11, 101
soldier 6, 7, 20, 25–6, 28, 59,
63–4, 67, 118
soliloquy 17, 33–4, 49–50,
53–4, 56, 59, 86
stage 5, 14–15, 17, 21–2, 25–7,
29, 31, 37, 39, 54, 84,
90–2, 94, 96, 101
Structuralism 47
Surrealists 21
symbol 40, 61, 72–3, 82, 88–9

theatre 2–3, 9, 41, 61, 87, 90,
96
tragedy 1, 36, 45, 47, 56,
89–90, 92, 108, 118–19,
121
tragic flaw 36
tragic hero 1
Traub, Valerie 43–7, 64, 68

Venice 1, 6–7, 11, 13, 15, 43,
60, 66, 68, 84, 93–5,
101, 109, 112, 117–18
verse 15, 17, 35, 53–4, 113
Wilson, Knight G. 89
Wimsatt, William K. 65
witchcraft 7, 15–16, 18, 22,
101

Yeats, William Butler 81